GOD WHERE ARE YOU?

I NEED YOU NOW!

I AM HERE

"When you search for me, you will find me; if you seek me with all your heart"

Jeremiah Chapter 29:13

Grace Dola Balogun

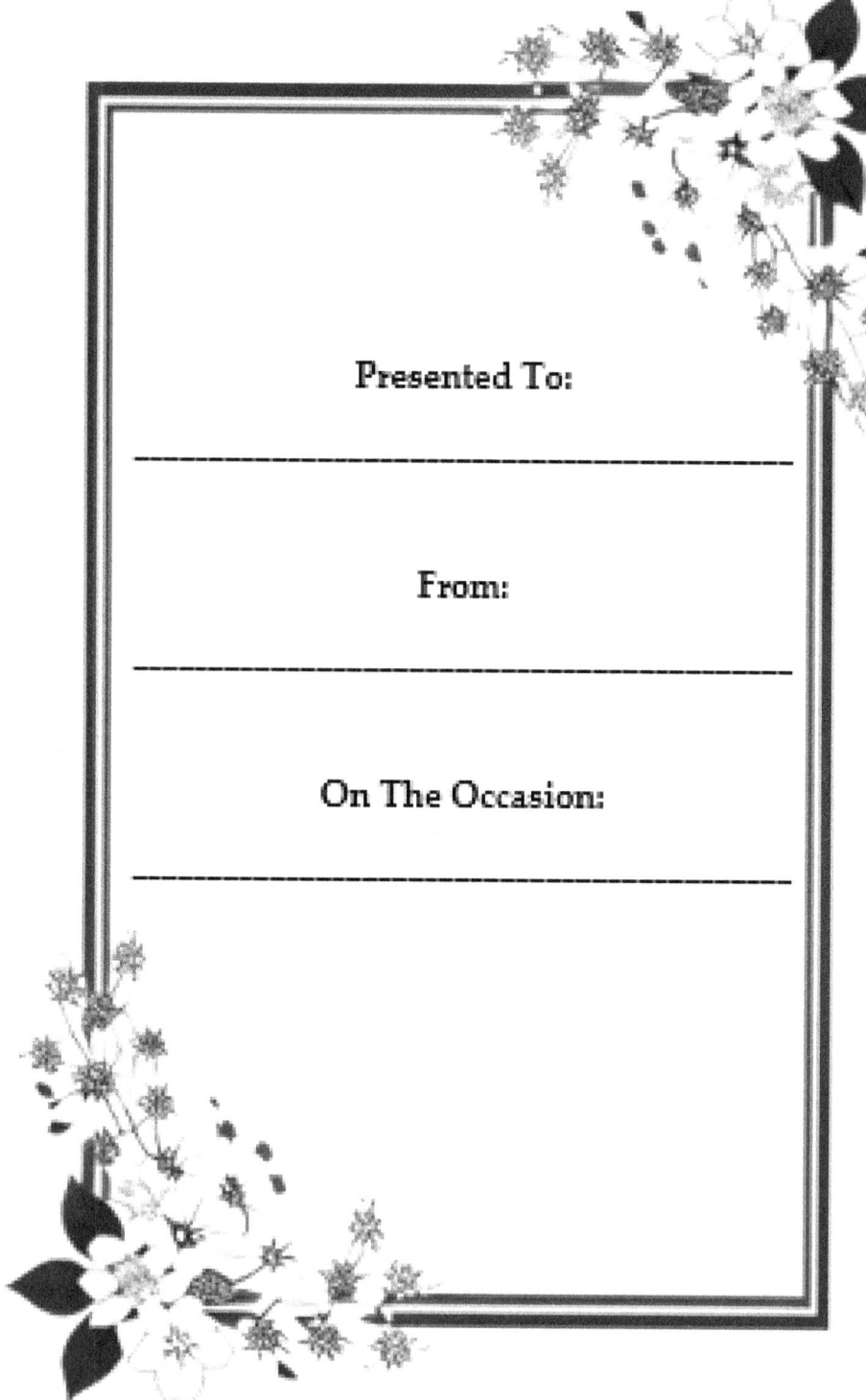

Copyright ©2024 Grace Dola Balogun

GOD WHERE ARE YOU?
By Grace Dola Balogun

Contact the Author at:
www.Gracereligiousbookspublishers.com

Business Office Phone: 1-203-891-7122

Grace Religious Books Publishing & Distributors, Inc.
New York

May be ordered through booksellers
or by contacting the publisher:
**Grace Religious Books Publishing & Distributors, Inc.
New York 248 Lombard Street 2nd Floor
New Haven, CT 06513**

All rights reserved. No part of this book may be used or reproduced by any means, graphic, electronic, or mechanical, including photocopying, recording, taping or by any information storage retrieval system without the written permission of the publisher except in the case of brief quotations embodied in critical articles and reviews. Because of the dynamic nature of the Internet, any web addresses or links contained in this book may have changed since publication and may no longer be valid. The views expressed in this work are solely those of the author and do not necessarily reflect the views of the publisher, and iii the publisher hereby disclaims any responsibility for them. author of this book does not dispense medical advice or prescribe the use of any technique for the treatment of physical, emotional, or medical problems without the advice of a physician, either directly or indirectly. The intent of the author is only to offer information of a general nature to help you in your quest for emotional and spiritual well-being. In the event you use any of the information in this book for yourself, which is your constitutional right, the author and the publisher assume no responsibility for your actions.

Scripture quotations marked (NIV) are taken from the Holy Bible, New International Version®, NIV®. Copyright © 1973, 1978, 1984, 2011 by Biblica, Inc.™ Used by permission of Zondervan. All rights reserved worldwide. www.zondervan.com. The "NIV" and "New International Version" are trademarks registered in the United States Patent and Trademark Office by Biblica, Inc.™

Soft Cover ISBN: 978-1-939415-98-1
Hard Cover ISBN: 978-1-963548-01-3

Library of Congress Control Number: 2024900449

Editing / Interior Book Design & Layout:

Grace Religious Books Publishing & Distributors, Inc.
New York

Printed in the United States of America

Dedication

In humble reverence, this book is devoted to God the Father Almighty, with gratitude for His boundless grace and unwavering presence. Seated at His right hand, Jesus Christ, the only Son, reigns in eternal unity with the Holy Spirit, forming the timeless triune God. Jesus, the great healer, holds the power to mend all afflictions and resolve life's myriad challenges, offering solace to every seeking soul.

May the words within these pages serve as a beacon, guiding those who ponder, "God, where are you?" toward a profound encounter with the Divine. As readers engage with the content, may their hearts be illuminated, inspiring a sincere quest for God, a quest fulfilled by the intimate connection of hearts, minds, spirits, souls, and bodies.

With a fervent prayer, let this book become a means through which individuals seek and discover the unchanging God, ever-present and eternal – the Lord God Almighty, Father, Son, and Holy Spirit, an indivisible unity. May it resonate as a transformative journey, leading all seekers to the realization that God, the constant and eternal One, is waiting to be found. Amen.

CONTENTS

Dedication iv

Preface 1

Chapter 1: Where is God In Time of Trouble? 4

Chapter 2: Where Is God In Time Of Tragedy? 14

Chapter 3: Where is God In Time of Sorrow? 28

Chapter 4: Where is God In Time of Loneliness? 44

Chapter 5: Where is God In Time of Need? ..56

Chapter 6: Where is God In Time of Anger? .67

Chapter 7: Where is God In Time of Immoralities? 81

Chapter 8: Where is God In Time of Imprisonment? 97

Chapter 9: Where Is God In Time Of Sickness & Diseases 111

Chapter 10: Where Is God In Time of War & Difficulties of Life? 135

Chapter 11: Humanity Rejected God 161

Chapter 12: Humanity Does Not Want To Know God 194

Summary 218

Prayer For Unbelievers And Believers 231

Song Of God of Creation 236

Revelation Our Lord .... **Error! Bookmark not defined.**

ORDER FORM 239

About the Author 240

Other Books by the Same Author 242

Page Blank Intentionally

Grace Dala Bolagun

Preface

Many people in this world do not want to hear the Word of God or know God until something uncomfortable happens in their lives, such as death in the family or the loss of their loved ones. Many people will like to tell you that they were atheists until sickness struck their bodies, tragedies such as fire, earthquake, disaster, war, volcano erupts, or mudslides.

Many people will tell you that they are still young and they do not want to find or know God until they are old to a certain age.

God Where Are You?

Some will say that if they know God, they will not be able to get rich or achieve what they want in life. They forget that nothing is beyond God's reach and that his purpose and plan sustain the entire world and all those who live in it. They don't believe that God is the source of their provisions. They don't want to know that Jesus Christ is the life and the light of the world. Jesus Christ told Tomas, one of his disciples: "I am the way and the truth and the life. Jesus is the way: He is the pathway to the Father. Jesus Christ is the truth: Christ is the revelation of who God is; Jesus Christ is the life: He is the risen Lord of life for all those who believe in him.

Believing means "believing by surrendering yourself to him in all you are doing and in all you do. Through Christ Jesus and with him and in him, we become the way, the truth, and the life. People always cry. Where is God when their lives turn around to what they do not expect; when all things are going their way, full of wealth, good health, and preposition, they don't ask the question, God, where are you? They don't want to let you even say "God Bless You" when they have a sinus infection, and since around you, "they will tell you don't say god Bless to me" because I am an Atheist." The people of this world must give their lives to God faithfully and sincerely before any problem comes into their lives so that they can be right there to receive help from the problem solver who can take care of their problems.

Chapter 1: Where is God In Time of Trouble?

When there was a plane crash that took the lives of many people on board, people asked where God was. And why can God not stop this plane crash before it Crashed? Is God still with us in this world? The Holy Scripture explained and clarified these questions: it revealed our sins; an example of King David's Story:

"The Lord sent Nathan to David. When

he came to him, he said there were two men in a certain town; one rich man had a very large number of sheep and cattle, but the poor man had nothing except one little Ewe-Lamb he had bought. He raised it, and it grew up with him and his children. It shaved his food, drank from his cup, and even slept in his arms. It was like a daughter to him. Now, a traveler came to the rich man, but the rich man refrained from taking one of his own sheep or cattle to prepare a meal for the traveler who had come to him. Instead, he took the Ewe-Lamb that belonged to the poor man and prepared it for the one who had come to him. David was turned with anger against the man and said to Nathan, as surely as the Lord lives, the man who did this deserves to die! He must pay for that Lamb four times over because he did such a thing and had no pity. Nathan said to David, You are the man! This is what the Lord, the God of Israel, says: I anointed you King over Israel, and I delivered you from the hand of Saul." I gave your master's house to you; I gave you all Israel and Judah. And if all this had been too little, I would have given you even more. Why did you despise the Word of the Lord by doing what is evil in his eyes? You struck down Uriah the Hittite with the sword and took his wife to be your own.

You killed him with the sword of the Ammonites. Now, therefore, the sword will never depart from your house because you despised me and took the wife of Uriah the Hittite to be your own." (2nd Samuel 12: 1-10)

Prophet Nathan declared to David that he had committed adultery, murder, and deceit. He was guilty of sin against God of despising the "word of the Lord," as well as despising God himself means he treated contemptuously, to scorn, to make little actions; by his actions, David was declaring God to be of little account, unworthy of love and devotion to the Lord God almighty.

In the church today, ministers of God who commit adultery reflect their estimate of God and his Holy Word. They treat the Gospel and the blood of Jesus Christ contemptuously, as if they are petty and unworthy of fidelity. The Holy Scripture states that any professed believer who enters into an adulterous relationship disqualifies himself from the office of overseer. The sin of humanity is the cause of all earthly troubles. Our sin of disobedient to the commandment of God leads the entire human race to all sorts of earthly trouble.

The Holy Scripture revealed that any professed Christian believer who enters or engages in an adulterous relationship disqualifies himself or herself from the ministry of the work of the Lord. Kind David said, in his confession, that when Nathan the prophet disclosed his sins of adultery and murder, David deliberately sinned against God. He feared that God's presence and Spirit would depart from him, leaving him spiritually destitute. David pleaded earnestly with God to restore fully the joy of his salvation, a pure heart, a spirit of persevering faith and obedience, and a testimony of praise. Sin opens the door for Satan to steal, kill, and destroy what is the most precious to us in our lives. All who have sinned greatly and are overwhelmed by feelings of guilt can find forgiveness, cleansing from their sins, and restoration through Jesus Christ, our redeemer King, if they boldly, sincerely, and faithfully approach God in Spirit and in truth. David's appeals for forgiveness and restoration are based on God's grace, mercy, unfailing love, and compassion when they are based on a truly broken heart and repentant heart and also ultimately on Jesus Christ's atoning death for our sins.

In the book of Psalms, the Scripture reveals: "Why, O Lord, Do you stand far off? Why do you hide yourself in times of trouble? In his arrogance, the wicked man hunts down the weak, who are caught in the schemes he devises. He boasts of the cravings of his heart; he blesses the greedy and reviles the Lord"

God Where Are You?

(Psalm 10:1-3). Many are questioning the apparent distance of the divine presence. It is suggested that this perceived separation is a result of humanity straying from God's commandments and the teachings of the Word. In our current era, injustice and malevolence seem to spread unchecked. At times, it appears as if God stands aloof, possibly because people only seek Him in prayer during moments of trouble, neglecting a deeper connection in their daily lives.

Some people have a haughty attitude of cruelty and wickedness, and because they were successful, they become more and more wicked. They don't want to know the salvation of the wicked; their sins and cruelty will never stop until they give their lives to Jesus Christ, who is able to give them new life in him after their confession of their sins. God almighty will soon abolish evil and all forms of evil that are spreading around the world. They have to know that God: "God is our refuge and strength, an ever-present help in trouble. Therefore, we will not fear though the earth gives way and mountain fall into the heart of the sea, though its waters roar and foam and the mountains quake with their surging" (Psalm 46:1-3) God the Father, God the Son, and God the Holy Spirit is our refuge and strength in the time of all the earthly trouble. Even though we all experience spiritual barrenness, sometimes this is not the norm, for God desires to be near to his people with all the help and comfort they may need. People of this world must express confidence and trust in the Lord during times of trouble, instability, and insecurity. The power and the ability to face life's uncertainties and adversities of life are found in the Lord Jesus; refuge will shelter his people from danger, indicating that God is our true security in the time of life's storms.

Strength comes from him because he will fight our battle without enemies, with his energy that works powerfully in us and enables us to overcome obstacles in life. The Lord God almighty Jesus Christ, the only Son, is ever-present and our helper in trouble. Lord God almighty is always available and always helps his children in times of trouble and in times of need. Jesus Christ is all-sufficient for any situation we might be going through; he never leaves our side; we must not be afraid or be afraid. God's river is the continual flow of his grace, glory, and power in the midst of his faithful people. This pure life-giving river flows from God the Father, God the Son, and God the Holy Spirit, forever one God; it flows from the throne of God and consistently refreshes all the believing Christians, both those on earth and as well as those in heaven. The most significant blessing of this river is that it brings God into the midst of his people, which means that the Lord Almighty is with us, the Holy Trinity, forever. One God is the source of our strength in any danger. He never leaves nor forsakes us, the most compassionate, most loving Savior and the Lord of all.

Chapter 2: Where Is God In Time Of Tragedy?

Human race believers and non-believers in this world always ask the questions: where is God, why is it that God let or allowed this tragedy to happen, and why did God allow tragedies in the life of humanity in this world? There are always never-ending tragedies in this world. Some tragedy is part of creation and nature. Other tragedies are violence, suspicion, hatred, and greed, which can cause tragedy when no one expects it. People always ask where God is when tragedy happens in our imperfect world.

Some people believe that tragedy is part of life in this world. There are so many events and tragedies in all the nations of this world. The tragedies that were caused by terrorists by, suicide bombers, by self-inflicted wounds. People always ask why God allowed it to happen when God is in the middle of the tragedy of life. Tragedy of wildfire whereby forty-thousand people lost their life and their homes as well as their properties. In the Old Testament in the book of Job, Job asked God when all his children died, World War II, the Holocaust, Genocides in Rwanda, the Soviet Union, China, Cambodia, Famines in African Nations, No clean water, New York World

Trade Center – 9/11 and presently Syrian slaughtering his people for the past 6-years sometimes with Chemical Weapon. Tragedy of Ebola and HIV, where people died of incurable diseases.

The Holy Scripture in the book of 1st Corinthian revealed: "Now we see but poor reflection as in a mirror; then we shall see face to face. Now I know in part; then I shall know fully, even as I am fully known" (1st Corrinthian13:12) "However, as it is written: No eye has seen, no ear has heard, no mind has conceived what God has prepared for those who love him" (1st Corinthian 2:9) God Almighty has nothing to do with the tragedies in the world.

When Adam and Eve sin, by disobeying God's commandment, they brought sin into the world and all forms of deadly accidents and murderous activities of human being that follows. Genesis 4:18, 2nd Corinthian 12:10, Matthew 24:7, Psalm 139:16, Daniels 4:34-35.

Hurricane Sandy and flood, Volcano Erupt. The Holy Scripture says that: "God saw all that he had made, and it was very good.

And there was evening, and there was morning - the sixth day" (Genesis 1:31). God, the creator of heaven and the earth, saw everything that he had created as very good. It is our sin that brought all forms of tragedies to all humankind. In another Scripture we read in the book of the second Samuel: "The waves of death swirled about me; the torrents of destruction overwhelmed me. The cords of the grave coiled around me; the snares of death confronted me. In my distress, I called to the

God Where Are You?

Lord; I called out to my God. From his temple he heard my voice; my cry came to his ears" (2nd Samuel 22:5-7). The Lord God almighty always hears our cry when we called unto him in the tragedies of life. The first tragedy of life happens when Adam and Eve lost their son Abel, and Cain, their first son, is jealous of Abel and kill him. It happened because Cain is the son of the devil from the Garden of Eden.

The devil is the one that introduced sex to Eve, and Eve introduced it to Adam. Therefore, Cain is the son of the devil called Satan. Abel is the natural son of Adam and Eve together in their intimate relationship that Eve introduced to Adam. The Holy Scripture revealed: "Adam lay with his wife Eve, and she became pregnant and gave birth to Cain.

She said, with the help of the Lord, I have

brought forth a man. Later, she gave birth to his brother Abel. Now Abel kept flocks, and Cain worked the soil. In the course of time, Cain brought some of the fruits of the soil has an offering to the Lord. But Abel brought fat portions from some of the firstborn of his flock. The Lord looked with favor on Abel and his offering, but on Cain and his offering, he did not look with favor. So Cain was very angry, and his face was downcast. Then the Lord said to Cain. Why are you angry? Why is your face downcast? But if you do not do what is right, sin is crouching at your door; it desires to have you, but you must master it. Now,, Cain said to his brother Abel. Let's go out to the field. And while they were in the field, Cain attacked his brother and kill him" (Genesis 4:1-8). Eve gave birth to her son; she gave sincere praise to the Lord for the child. She was seeking to be rightly related to God in thankfulness for his love, forgiveness, and help. The Lord accepted Abel's offering because he came before God in true faith and dedication to His righteousness. Cain, on the other hand, was rejected his offering because his deeds were evil.

God takes pleasure in our offerings and thanksgivings only when we are striving to live a righteous life according to his will. God looks at sin as a tempting, ready to attack and devour. Yet God, in his grace, also gives to the human being the capacity to overcome and resist sin by submitting to his Word, with the assistance of his Spirit.

It is their choice whether they will yield to sin or will conquer it. Adam and Eve cried uncontrollably for the tragic death of their son,

Abel.

As well as cried for the evil that Cain committed by killing his own brother. The Scripture revealed: " Then the Lord said to Cain, where is your brother Abel? I don't know, he replied.

Am I my brother's keeper? The Lord said, what have you done? Listen! Your brother's blood cries out to me from the ground. Now, you are under a curse and driven from the ground, which opened its mouth to receive your brother's blood from your hand. When you work the ground, it will no longer yield its crops for you. You will be a restless wanderer on earth. Cain said to the Lord my punishment is more than I can bear.

Today, you are driving me from the land, and I will be hidden from your presence; I will be a restless wanderer on the earth, and whoever finds me will kill me" (Genesis 4:9-14). The death of Abel and God's concern for him show that throughout the ages, God, almighty Father, cared for all who suffered because of their commitment to righteousness.

Their suffering is always known to God, the holy trinity, and he will one day act on their behalf to render justice and destroy all evil. Cain was cursed by God in the sense that God would no longer bless his efforts to gain his living from the ground. Evidently, Cain did not humble himself, in godly sorrow and repentance, for what he did, the sin of committing murder; he separated himself from the Lord and sought to live without God's help. Scripture revealed: "But the Lord said to him, not so, if anyone kills Cain, he will suffer vengeance seven times over. The Lord put a mark on Cain so that no one who found him would kill him, so Cain went out from the Lord's presence and lived in the land of Nod, East of Eden" (Genesis 4:15-16). This can be easily understood in the sense of a sign given to Cain to assure him of God's promise. The death penalty was not carried out on Cain. Capital punishment came later when the wickedness and violence of the human race became very great on the earth. The Lord God Almighty Father, Son and Holy Spirit, God of love and who full of mercy, did not put the death penalty on Cain, or allow anyone to kill him. He was the first man on earth to commit tragedy by killing his own brother. The nations should read this S cripture and cancel the judgment of the death penalty in some states of America and in other nations of the world. The Scripture revealed: "And we know that in all things God works for the good of those who love him, who have been called according to his purpose" (Romans 8:28). This is the Scripture often offers encouragement for all those who go and are going through tragedy. It greatly encourages God's children, his people, when they must endure suffering in this life. God will bring good out of all tragedies and afflictions, trials, persecutions, and suffering; the good that God's works are conforming us to the image of Christ, ultimately bringing about our glorification. This promise is for those who love God and have submitted to him through faith in Christ. The 'all things" do not include our sins and negligence; no one can excuse sin by maintaining that God will work it out for good. Jesus Christ's commandments entail much more than doing this or avoiding that or the other. We keep Jesus' commandments by living his way of life, a life that is characterized by a deep care for others. His commandments are to love as he loved, believe as he believed, and live as he lived.

Christ's commandments are the most self-engaging and most challenging of all! How comforting, then, when Christ Jesus says, "I will not leave you as orphans." No, we are not orphans. The risen Lord Jesus Christ comes to us. You will ask how in the Spirit of truth and righteousness. The Scripture in the book of Ecclesiastes says: "He has made everything beautiful in its time. He has also set eternity in the hearts of men, yet they cannot fathom what

God has done from beginning to end. I know that there is nothing better for men than to be happy and do good while they live. That everyone may eat and drink and find satisfaction in all his toil – this is the gift of God. I know that everything God does will endure forever; nothing can be added to it, and nothing can be taken from it. God does it so that men will revere him" (Ecclesiastes 3:11-14). God placed within the human heart an inherent desire for more than just the earthly. Human beings want to live forever and find eternal value in the world and the activities of life. Consequently, material things, secular activities, and the pleasures of this earth will never be satisfied. The gift of God through Jesus Christ our Lord is the ability to enjoy life and live it properly. It is a gift of God that comes only when we are brought into the right relationship with him and sincerely submit ourselves to him as our Lord and God.

He will then give us joy in all that we do or say. When tragedy comes, he will help us to deal with it and lessen the sorrow and sadness of tragedy.

Chapter 3: Where is God In Time of Sorrow?

There is always a time of sorrow for everyone on this earth. Believing Christians are not exempt from sorrow, painful situations, and circumstances. However, because of the indwelling power of the Holy Spirit, we have hope that keeps us from one moment to another moment at a time, because sorrow is not an easy thing to go through, but with the grace and mercy of God in our life, we always overcome any form of sorrow. The Scripture says: "At time to weep and a time laugh, a time to mourn and a time to dance" (Ecclesiastes 3:4). This Scripture explains that there will be a time of sorrow; we cannot escape it because of sin that is in the world. The sinfulness of humanity and actions will bring sorrow to the people of this world until Jesus Christ returns and sets up his kingdom of peace and righteousness.

Christian believers must know that our sorrow is already known to our Father in Heaven, Jesus Christ, his only Son, and Holy Spirit, forever one God. Jesus Christ always helps us in the time of our sorrow; he strengthens us spiritually and physically during the time of our sorrow, and our hope is in the Lord.

God Where Are You?

As the Scripture says, there is a time for everything and for every season under heaven. God almighty has an eternal plan that includes the purpose and activities of every person on this earth. We must give ourselves to God as Holy sacrifices and allow the Holy Spirit to accomplish God's plan for us, and we must be careful not to be out of God's plan for us and be careful not to be out of God's will and miss His timing and purpose for our lives. God the Father Almighty has set eternity in the hearts of men. He has placed within the human hearts an inherent desire for more than just the earthly. Humanity wants to live forever and find eternal value in this world and in the activities of life. Consequently, all the material things of the world, and all the secular activities and the pleasure of this earth will never be fully satisfied. The Scripture revealed: "It is better to go to a house of mourning than to go to a house of feasting, for death is the destiny of every man; the living should take this to heart. Sorrow is better than laughter because a sad face is good for the heart" (Ecclesiastes 7:2-3). When we are comforting those who are going through sorrowful times, we are also reminding ourselves of all the problems of this world and the promise of heaven; it helps us to strengthen and place our total lives with God's will and his purposes for our lives. It helps us to focus on how we can be fruitful and be in pursuit of the holiness and righteousness of God. The time of sorrow placed in us the reality that we must be ambassadors for Christ on this earth, and we are all here temporarily. Heaven is our home.

King Solomon contracts the sober effects of sorrow and the grief caused by a wise rebuke with the laughter and frivolous joking of fools. Those who are reprimanded may feel sad, but such sorrow often results in their repentance; because they are now confronted with the real issues of life, such sorrow is better than laughter and good times. Christian believers see many tears running through the darkness of sorrow and pain; however, through the love and the light of Christ, we can be joyful in the middle of sorrow. Sorrow always has an end because the Scripture says: "For his anger lasts only a moment, but his favor lasts a lifetime; weeping may remain for a night, but rejoicing comes in the morning" (Psalm 30:5-6). When I felt Secure, I said, I will never be shaken." God almighty is always in control of our sorrows and the causes of our sorrows. The Lord will not let his people be in a constant state of sadness, sorrow, and weeping.

This is the reason why he fills us with the Holy Spirit, who dwells in us and who is the translator of our groaning and moaning into prayers and sends them to heaven for us. Our Lord is also the source of our peace and helps us to endure afflictions during difficult days so that we can be able to go through our times of sorrow with his victory. Christian believers felt secure, secure in their prosperity. The psalmist assumed that his wealth and success made him so strong that nothing could destroy his happiness. God then withdrew his protective hand and brought serious trouble and helplessness into his life, causing him to experience the need for God's continual care and presence. All believers who feel secure in themselves, who rely on temporal things, and who give God and his Kingdom anything but the first place in their lives are warned by the words of this Scripture. In another Scripture, we read: "My soul is warty with sorrow strengthen me according to your word" (psalm 119:28). Believing Christians must pray continually to God almighty through the power of the Holy Spirit so that they can draw near to God in the time of sorrow, in order to increase their knowledge and understanding of our sources of sorrow and teach us his truth to overcome it.

Sorrow can make us weary and feel hopeless, but without prayer and supplication, we will be strengthened in him.

The Holy Scripture revealed: "You turned my wailing into dancing; you removed my sackcloth and clothed me with joy, that my heart may sing to you and not be silent. O Lord my God, I will give you thanks forever" (Psalm 30:11-12) The people of this world as well as the Christian believers they can easily be lost during the time of their sorrow and it might even encompass their entire lives. But to those who put their trust in the Lord, those who gave their Spirit, soul, and body in total surrender and put their hope in Jesus Christ our Lord – The time of sorrow, or in the season of sorrow, they will receive the faithfulness of our Lord and Savior and the love of God will be demonstrated with joy in the Holy Spirit in their lives. For those who know and belong totally to Jesus Christ, there will always be a day of rejoicing because the joy of the Lord will be their strength forever. When sorrow ears a Christian believer down, it is very important to keep their heart and mind focused on the Lord and in his Word by constantly reading the Scripture, meditating on his Word, and by unceasing prayers to the Father, Son, and Holy Spirit.

The time of sorrow is when believing Christians need to get closer and closer to the Lord for his help, mercy, and love. The Scripture revealed in the Book of Revelation:

"And I heard a loud voice from the throne saying, Now, the dwelling of God is with men, and he will live with them.

They will be his people, and God himself will be with them and be their God. He will wipe every tear from their eyes. There will be no more death or mourning or crying or pain, for the old order of things has passed away" (Revelation 21:3-4). God the Father almighty will wipe every tear, and there will be no more sorrow in the new heaven and in the new earth among his own people; the believer's Solid Rock is Jesus Christ. He is our hope of glory, the God of comfort, the sustainer of all things, and the restorer of all things; he will restore us from the bondage of sorrow. Jesus Christ is our blessed hope of glory in a new heaven and a new earth – he is our final goal; our expectation of all the redeemed is a new, transformed, and redeemed world where Jesus Christ will live with his people and righteousness dwell in holy perfection. He will erase all the traces of sin, and sorrow, pain;

there will be a destruction of the earth, stars, and galaxies; heaven and earth will be shaken and will vanish like smoke. The stars will be dissolved, and the elements destroyed. The new earth will become the dwelling place of both humanity and God. All the redeemed will possess bodies like Christ's resurrection body, ones that are real, visible, and tangible but incorruptible and immortal. Jesus Christ will wipe every tear from our eyes; the effects of sin, such as sorrow, pain, unhappiness, and death, will be gone forever, for the evil things of the first heaven and earth have completely passed away. Christian believers, although remembering all things worth remembering, will evidently not remember that which would cause them sorrow. The Lord God almighty said in the book of Isaiah:

Grace Dala Bolagun

"Behold, I will create new heavens and a new earth. The former things will not be remembered, nor will they come to mind. But be glad and rejoice forever in what I will create, for I will create Jerusalem to be a delight and its people a joy. I will rejoice over Jerusalem and take delight in my people; the sound of weeping and of crying will be heard in it no more. Never again will there be in it an infant who lives but a few days or an old man who does not live out his years; he who dies at a hundred will be thought a mere youth; He who fails to reach a hundred will be considered accursed" (Isaiah 65: 17-20) This prophecy of the prophet Isaiah foresees God's future Kingdom on earth prophet Isaiah blends the age of eternity where sin and death will be no more with the Messianic age- the millennial

Kingdom that precedes it begins with a strong adversative; but there will indeed be new heavens and a new earth, but od also has plans for the present Jerusalem in his millennial Kingdom where only righteous dwell infants who live for few days, although death will still exist in the Messianic Kingdom, the life span will be much longer than what they are now. A Hundred years will still be considered a youth, and those who die before that age will be considered accursed. God himself declares who will inherit the blessings of the new heaven and the new earth – those who faithfully persevere as Jesus Christ's overcomers. Those who do not overcome Satan, sin, and ungodliness will be thrown into the fiery lake. The Scripture in the book of Matthew says: "Blessed are those who mourned, for they will be comforted" (Matthew 5:4). The Lord almighty comforted those who are mourning, those who are weak in relation to God's standard of righteousness and his Kingdom power. Christians also mourn over the things that grieve God, to have our feelings in sympathy with the feelings of God, and to be afflicted in our spirits over the sin, immorality, and cruelty manifested in the world.

Those who mourn are comforted by receiving from the Father the righteousness, peace, and joy in the Holy Spirit. During the time of sorrow, we do not feel the blessings of the Lord, but we know that he is the God of all comfort. He is always comforting us. The Scripture revealed: "Godly sorrow brings repentance that leads to salvation and leaves no regret, but worldly sorrow brings death. See what this godly sorrow has produced in you: What earnestness, what eagerness to clear yourselves, what indignation, what alarm, what longing, what concern, what readiness to see justice done. At every point you have proved yourselves to be innocent in this matter" (2nd Corinthian 7:10-11). Apostle Paul identifies two different kinds of sorrow in this Scripture: (1) There is a genuine sorrow for sin that leads to repentance, which means a change of heart and mind that causes us to turn from sin to God. This type of repentance leads people of this world to salvation.

    Paul knows that repentance from sin and faith in the Lord Jesus Christ are human being's responsibilities for salvation. There are two distinct differences between the godly sorrow and the sorrow of the world.

Apostle Peter was sorrowful because he denied the Lord three times; he repented and returned to the disciples in the Upper-room and continued to minister together: but we see Judas Iscariot who was sorrowful for handling the Lord to the leaders of the Pharisees and Seduces, he did not repent, and he committed suicide by hanging himself on the tree. Godly sorrow brings repentance to our knees in complete surrender to the Lord Jesus Christ.

Whereas worldly sorrow only offers a temporary relief that leads to death and sin, sin and death.

Chapter 4: Where is God In Time of Loneliness?

The people of this world struggle with loneliness at one time or another.

Whether they are going through something in their lives that makes them feel that they are the only ones going through such loneliness or whether they are going through some changes in their lives and feel alone, the word of God provides hope and blesses us in times of loneliness. Jesus Christ is our true friend. With him in our lives, we will never feel alone. Christ is closer to us than anyone in this world. He is a true friend that never fails, and he will never fail us; all we need to do is to focus on him. Loneliness was the first that God said that it is not good according to the Holy Scripture revealed: "God made the wild animals according to their kinds, the livestock according to their kinds and all the creatures that move along the ground according to their kinds.

And God saw that it was good. Then God said, let us make man in our image, in our likeness, and let them rule over the fish of the Sea and the birds of the air, over the livestock, over all the earth, and over all the creatures that move along the ground. So God created man in his own image in the image of God he created him; male and female he created them" (Genesis 1:25-27). The Lord God said, it is not good for the man to be alone, I will make a helper suitable for him" (Genesis 2:18) Then the Lord God made a woman from the rib he had taken out of the man, and brought her to the man. The man said, this is now bone of my bones and flesh of my flesh; she shall be called woman, for she was taken out of man" (Genesis 2:22-23). God almighty created males and females in his own image in order to work together for the glory of God. God brought Eve to Adam. He knows that all animals, birds, and all other creations have a partner, but Adam is the only one without a helper or companion. He needs contact with another human being; Eve will share in the joy of the Lord in the Garden of Eden, Adam will have someone like him to talk to besides the other creatures, such as animals and birds, and Eve will share in the wonders and power of God creations as well as in the responsibilities of stewardship Eve was created to be a loving companion for Adam and a helper in the work of the Lord.

Eve was to share with Adam; she must cooperate with him in fulfilling God's purpose for his life and the life of their family. Everyone on this earth experiences a season of loneliness or isolation in so many ways; people on this earth overcome loneliness by joining Clubs, friends, or social events. Loneliness does not happen or develop in one day; it can be a result of rejection, disappointment, or other lifetime circumstances that influence our personality; trauma can easily move one into total isolation, whereby they can no longer trust anyone with their life. Many people live a life of loneliness because of what they went through at the early age of their lives. Unmarried people, widows, and devoiced people might be struggling with loneliness because of the problem of devoicing and the cost of loved ones. God almighty does not want anyone to be lonely; he wants us to share our lives with the love of God with other people. The Scripture in the Old Testament reveals: "Be strong and courageous. Do not be afraid or terrified because of them, for the Lord your God goes with you; he will never leave you nor forsake you" (Deuteronomy 31:6). This is one of the Scriptures of encouragement during the time of loneliness that gave us the word of assurance of the ever-present of the Lord in our lives. This is the promise of God that never fails for those people on this earth who sincerely receive Jesus Christ as their Lord and Savior.

Christian believers are assured that if they love God above all else and depend on him instead of depending on material security, the Lord will never desert nor forsake them, but he will be their helper. Therefore, because of God's promise, we must not allow loneliness to overpower us; we must be strong and courageous, persevering in trials, afflictions, and tribulations; we must be strong to resist any temptations, persecutions, trusting in the love of God, which is in Christ Jesus and fully obedient to his words. The Book of Romans revealed: "What, then, shall we say in response to this? If God is for us, who can be against us? He who did not spare his own Son but gave him up for us all, how will he not also, along with him, graciously give us all things? Who will bring any charge against those whom God has chosen? It is God who justifies. Who is he that condemns? Christ Jesus, Who died – more than that, who was raised to life – is at the right hand of God and is also interceding for us. Who shall separate us from the love of Christ? Shall trouble or hardship or persecution or famine or nakedness or danger or sword? As it is written: For your sake, we face death all day long; we are considered as sheep to be slaughtered; no, in all these things, we are more than conquerors through him who loved us. For I am convinced that neither death nor life, neither angels nor demons, neither the present nor the future, nor any powers, neither height nor depth, nor anything else in all creation will be able to separate us from the love of God that is in Christ Jesus our Lord" (Romans 8:31-39) Christian believers must rejoice with these words of assurance, those who gave their life to Jesus Christ there is no lonely lives, and they will never be lonely because of Jesus Christ heavenly intercession in their lives. All the believers' adversities that is the experience of God's people in all generations.

Believers should not think that it is strange if they experience trouble, loneliness, persecution, hunger, poverty, or danger.

Trouble and calamity do not necessarily mean that God has deserted them or that he has stopped loving them. On the contrary, our suffering as Christian believers will open up the way by which we experience more of God's love and comfort. We will overcome all the adversities, and we will be more than conquerors through Jesus Christ. The Lord of God, which is Christ Jesus our Lord and Savior, surpasses all understanding.

If anyone fails in their spiritual life, it will neither be from a lack of divine grace and love nor from external force or over-whelming g adversity, but from their own neglect to remain in Christ Jesus; only in Christ Jesus is God's love and mercy manifested, revealed, and only in him do we experience his love. Only as we remain in Christ Jesus as our Lord and Savior can we have the certainty of life that we will never be separated from the love of God, which is in Christ Jesus our Lord. In the middle of life, we are more than conquerors, which means we are over, above, victors and conquerors. Apostle Paul says that instead of believers seeing themselves as victims in this fallen world, in Jesus Christ, we are over and above victors; instead, we see ourselves barely getting by in life's difficult experiences, and through Jesus Christ, we are overwhelmingly conquerors. Jesus Christ gained and got the decisive victory for us at the cross. Because of his victory and the power of the Holy Spirit within us, we are empowered to be more than conquerors in all our struggles in life. There is loneliness in the lives of those who faithfully truthfully gave their lives to the Father, the Son, and the Holy Spirit on this earth; they will never be alone. Christ's word is final: "I will never leave you nor forsake you."

Another Holy Scripture that revealed there is no loneliness in the lives of people of God: "And I will do whatever you ask in my name, so that the Son may bring glory to the Father And I will ask the Father, and he will give you another Counselor to be with you forever" (John 14:13, 16) In our time of loneliness Jesus Christ wants us to come to him in prayer, he said we should ask in his name. Prayer in Jesus' name involves at least two things: (1) praying in harmony with his nature, character, and will. (2) Praying with faith in him and his authority and with the desire to glorify both the Father and the Son. Praying in the name of Jesus Christ, therefore, means that Jesus Christ will answer any prayer that he would have prayed himself. There is no limit to the power of prayer when addressed to Jesus or the Father in holy faith according to his desire. Jesus Christ will ask the Father to give that counselor only to those who are serious about their love for him and their devotion to his word. Jesus uses the present tense, where he emphasizes a continuing attitude of love and obedience. The counselor, the Holy Spirit, will be by the disciples' side to help and strengthen them, to teach them the true course of their lives, to comfort them in difficult situations, to intercede for them in prayer for them, to be a friend to further their best interest and to remain with them forever, you see clearly that there is no loneliness in the life of a child of God.

Chapter 5: Where is God In Time of Need?

God Almighty Father of all mercies, the sustainer of all things, maker of heaven and earth, promised to supply all our needs if we can trust him and come to him in time of our needs and put all that we need in his holy hands; he is faithful and to supply all our needs. All the believing Christians must come to Jesus Christ, who is the supplier of all our needs. There are no problems that are too tough, no petition too inconsequential, and no power too transcendent for him to handle. Jesus Christ is our Great High Priest in heaven. He will solve all our problems and fulfill all our needs at the right time, at the correct timing, with his power, mercy, and great compassion.

The Scripture revealed: "Fear the Lord, you, His Saints, for those who fear him lack nothing.

The Lions may grow weak and hungry, but those who seek the Lord lack no good thing" (Psalm 34:9-10 God almighty Father, Son, and Holy Spirit promise his children a conditional reserved which is only for those who genuinely fear the Lord Jesus Christ our Lord and Savior promises to deliver us from fear of in need of food and clothing, he saves us from trouble, he sends his holy angels to encamp around us and supply all our needs. Jesus Christ gives us abundant life so that we will not lack anything; the Lord hears our prayers as we cry to him for our needs in prayers every day.

Jesus Christ is all-sufficient and the God of comfort; he comforts us with his presence every time we call unto him to redeem us from our past, present, and future sins. The most important thing he required from us was that we must seek the Lord, cry out to him in times of our needs, we must draw close to him, fear him, keep our tongues from lying, remain separated from the evil work, do good to people and pursue peace we must have a contrite hearts and become his servants, his disciples. Our Lord was teaching during his earthly ministry and said: "So do not worry, saying, what we shall eat? Or what shall we drink? Or what shall we wear? For the pagans run after all these things, and your heavenly Father knows that you need them" (Matthew 6:31-32) God the Father knows what we needed, and he has the power and authority to provide our needs. He gave us his word; he said we should not worry about our needs. He wants us to seek his face continually above all our earthly needs. God promised to provide for our food, clothing, and all the necessities. We must not worry if we let him reign in our lives; let him take total control and assume full responsibility when we fully and wholly yield to His Lordship. The Scripture revealed in the book of Joshua: "Do not let this book of the Law depart from your mouth; meditate on it day and night, so that you may be careful to do everything written in it. Then, you will be prosperous. Have I not commanded you? Be strong and courageous, do not be terrified; do not be discouraged, for the Lord your God will be with you wherever you go" (Joshua 1:8-9). Our Lord wants us to be prosperous and successful in everything we do, are doing, or are going to do. Those who know and obey God's word and law will be prosperous and successful in that they possess the wisdom to live righteously and to achieve God's goal for their lives. The requirements for prosperity and success are: (1) Be strong, courageous, and diligent. (2) Make God's word your authoritative guide for all your beliefs and actions. (3) Study the Holy Scriptures and meditate daily on God's Word. (4) Determine to seek God's presence throughout your life earnestly.

This message that the Lord God gave to Joshua is for all the Christian believers today until Christ returns, the message of Joshua to us Christians today provides us with a set of general principles for successful living; we must be sure that God will do more abundantly, exceedingly to everyone who follows his conditions, and these general principles are not guarantees, for they are subject to God's higher standard choices for each of us; sometimes, God permits us to undergo suffering and adversity in order to be strong in him and to enjoy our successful lives. Scripture revealed: "For the Lord God is a sun and shield; the Lord bestow us favor and honor; no good things does he withhold from those whose walk is blameless" (Psalm 84:11). Our Lord and Savior's love is incomparable, incomprehensible, no good thing does he withhold from those who diligently seeking him and gave their life to him. His promise is directed explicitly to all the Christian believers who sincerely strive to live godly and righteous lives. What God regards as good relates directly to fulfilling his purpose for our lives. Our task is to walk uprightly and to trust God to furnish everything that is good for us physically and spiritually, temporarily and eternally. The Lord has the power and authority to fulfill all our needs. The Scripture revealed: "But I will restore you to health and heal your wounds, declares the Lord because you are called an outcast, Zion for whom no one cares" (Jeremiah 30:17). God Almighty is the God of provisions. He has the power and love to restore his people, those who are in need of healing in so many areas of their bodies, to good health. He will heal their wounds; he is the great physician, the great healer, and he will bless them with good health. Those people who think they are nothing and cannot be anything, people without homes, will provide shelter for them; they will begin a new life in him because no one loves them like him and no one cares for them like him.

He is the God of love, God of great compassion. He is always there for us and supplies all our needs. The Scripture revealed: "And my God will meet all your needs according to his glorious riches in Christ Jesus. To our God and Father be glory forever and ever. Amen." (Philippians 4:19-20) Apostle Paul was assuring believers then and us today that God is the leading supplier of all our needs according to his riches and glory. Paul emphasizes the loving care of God the Father for his children.

He will meet all our needs, both material needs as well as our spiritual needs, if we present all our needs to him.

He will meet them in Christ Jesus our Lord, his only begotten Son. Only through our life and union with Jesus Christ and in his fellowship, can we experience God's provisions among the many promises of the word of God that give us hope and encouragement, all Christian believers, concerning his care for us and his help for us never fail.

Scripture reveals: "I am with you and will watch over you wherever you go, and will bring you back to this land. I will not leave you until I have done what I have promised you" (Genesis 28:15). God almighty always keep his promises God came to Jacob with the message that the blessing promised to Abraham would be carried on to completion through him. With this blessing came the promise of God's presence, guidance, and protection. The Scripture revealed: "The Lord your God has blessed you in all the work of your hands.

He has watched over your journey through this vast desert. These forty years the Lord your God has been with you, and you have not lacked anything" (Deuteronomy 2:7). God almighty Father was telling the children of Israel that for the past forty years that they have been in the wilderness, he has never leave them nor forsake them that, he always supply their needs. Although the Israelites had to pay for their sins of unbelief and rebellion, God continued, in a measure, to be with them because they confessed their sin. God will continue to bless and guide those who repent and give their lives to him, in spite of their failures and their temporary departure from a life of holiness according to God's word.

Chapter 6: Where is God In Time of Anger?

The cure to anger is the reading of the Word of God; Christian believers must let the Word of God dwell in them richly. All God's Children must change and get rid of sinful anger. Understanding and applying the word of truth, which is the word of God, to your life will help you overcome sinful anger and live a peaceful life. People must surrender their anger to God the Holy Spirit, and anger can be righteous. The Scripture says: "In your ANGER DO NOT SIN.

Do not let the sun go down while you are still angry, and do not give the devil a foothold" (Ephesians 4:26-27). Christians must avoid sinning in the heat of anger. God's people should not nurse, rehearse, or discuss their anger, nor should they project it onto others. Instead, they should control their anger and deal with it quickly to prevent the enemy from gaining any ground in their hearts. Anger could be a fruit; anger could be false in worship service by expressing anger in a sinful way. Anger is a domineering sin to a sinner; Jesus Christ's blood of righteousness covers the sinner's anger: Romans 6:5-11, 1st Corinthian 6:9-11 The Scripture deals with anger problems. There is always anger in a relationship that leads to a grave sin.

There are three different angers in every human being. Anger destroys marriage. Believing Christians must put their anger, get rid of anger, and any form of abusive speech from their mouth. They must be able to control their anger because anger can lead to death. Examine yourself and find out if your anger is righteous, sinful, or both. Christian believers must be able to control their sinful anger through the power of the indwelling of the Holy Spirit that lives in them. They must confess all their manners and activities of their sinful anger towards people.

We live in a world that is full of anger from the household to the parliament and congress of the nations. Anger in politics: most of the entertainment industry's movies are full of rage and anger towards each other or about material things of the world. Television family shows display anger, with mothers and fathers screaming and yelling at each other, grown-up children, and siblings yelling at each other with rage and anger.

Anger full our Sports, which is supposed to be a friendly gesture. Anger is expressed daily in the business, corporate, state, and federal offices in the nation. Anger and rage are expressed in all our daily newspapers. Nations threaten other countries because of anger and violence.

The Holy Scripture is telling humanity every day of anger. Anger has many ways of its causes and can be expressed in many ways. There is what they call explosive and blow-up anger, which some people express expect and which can result in murder within a second when the person explodes with anger. It is like a time Bomb; it happens in two people's relationship. It is sinful, selfish, and prideful. It could happen in traffic between two drivers, and before you know it, one is dead. Many in this world struggle with all types of anger in their lives; it happens between husband and wife because of something that one said before. It can be resolved if the other opponent is not dead; they will be filing for a divorce. A man shoots and kills his wife because his wife is laughing at something that he did wrong; he is in the rage of anger and kills his wife in front of their children, causing all his children a lifetime of sorrow. People express anger because the other party is silent about their problem, and they become angry and full of anger, which immediately destroys the relationship between them. Anger destroys relationships with friends, family, relatives, business partners, and the political arena. Silent anger is a destroyer, just as explosive anger. There is also an irritating or bitter anger that hurts and damages the lives of those who struggle with it. Anger is a threat to those who exercise it, and the person that they are angry with could be a coworker, a friend, a relative, or a family friend.

Anger damages the love of God in every individual. The Holy Scripture revealed the problem and how dangerous anger is. Anger was exercised in the Garden of Eden, and it will continue to destroy human lives until Jesus Christ returns to earth.

Humanity's anger was expressed when

they intentionally disobeyed God and listened to Satan, who told them that they should do whatever or eat whatever was good in their own eye. The Scripture says that the Lord God almighty revealed himself to Moses: "And he passed in front of Moses, proclaiming the Lord, the Lord, the compassionate and gracious God, slow to anger, abounding in love and faithfulness, maintaining love to thousands and forgiving wickedness, rebellion and sin" (Exodus 34:6-7) The Lord God the Compassionate gracious loving God never angry with no one no matter how sinful we are. The Lord is a great God whose compassion, kindness, and forgiveness are united with truth, holiness, and justice. God almighty is gracious and compassionate, showing that he will punish anyone who takes the law into their hand and revenger with anger towards another to destroy the other or murder them with the rage of anger.

Parents and the people of this earth must take note that their sins, spiritual neglect, or failure to separate themselves from the ungodliness of the world can have tragic consequences for their children or the younger generations. Children suffer for the sins of their parents in the sense that they generally follow their parents along the path of the temptation of rage and anger or spiritual compromise, thereby adopting evil habits of anger and destruction as well as attitudes that will lead them away from God which will end up leading them to lives of destruction. Anger and rage are a life that is ruled by sin and full of sinful nature. Many people become addicted to the lives of anger, and they are controlled by their anger.

The Scripture says: "Do not know that the wicked will not inherit the Kingdom of God? Do not be deceived: Neither the sexually immoral nor idolaters nor adulterers nor male prostitutes nor homosexual offenders nor thieves nor the greedy nor drunkards nor slanderers nor swindlers will inherit the Kingdom of God.

And that is what some of you were.

But you were washed, you were sanctified, you were justified in the name of the Lord Jesus Christ and by the Spirit of our God" (1st Corinthian 6:9-11). The wicked person who is full of rage and anger will not inherit the Kingdom of God. Justification involves both the redemptive work of the grace of the Lord

Jesus Christ and the work of the Holy Spirit.

In another Scripture: "My dear brothers, take note of this: everyone should be quick to listen, slow to speak and slow to become angry, for man's anger does not bring about the righteous life that God desires" (James 1:19-20) God almighty commands us to get rid of anger in order to live a righteous life that the Lord requires from all the people that came to this world. In another Scripture: "The Lord is compassionate and gracious, slow to anger, abounding in love. He will not always accuse, nor will he harbor his anger forever" (Psalm 103:8-9). Our Lord and Savior shows mercy to those who fear him. The fear of God is a redeeming fear that motivates us to turn away from evil and to keep God's Commandment and his word in our hearts. "A fool gives full vent to his anger, but a wise man keeps himself under control" (Proverbs 29:11). "In your anger do not sin; when you are on your beds search your hearts and be silent" (Psalm4:4). In another Scripture: "In your anger do not sin; Do not let the sun go down while you are still anger, and do not give the devil a foothold. He who has been stealing must steal no longer but must work, doing something useful with his own hands so that he may have something to share with those in need. Do not let any unwholesome talk come out of your mouth, but only what is helpful for building others up according to their needs, that it may benefit those who listen.

And do not grieve the Holy Spirit of God, with whom you were sealed for the day of redemption. Get rid of all bitterness, rage and anger, brawling and slander, along with every form of malice. Be kind and compassionate to one another, forgiving each other; just as in Christ God forgave you" (Ephesians 4:26-32). The Lord God made it clear and précised to stay away from bitterness, wrath, rage, and anger that those Christian believers who were redeemed but still practice those things are grieving the Holy Spirit who lives within them.

Grieving the Holy Spirit always leads to resisting the Holy Spirit, which will, in the end, lead to putting out the Spirit's fire and finally insulting the Spirit of grace. This is the reason the Scripture says to be angry but not let your anger turn to sin. There is a righteous anger that could be expressed by a believing Christian. Our Lord gave his life for us on the Calvary Tree when the people got angry and nailed him to the cross. Christ died and rose again in order to free us from the sinful nature of anger; during your anger towards someone, express righteous anger without sin. Jesus Christ's blood covers and wash away all our anger, our rage, our bitterness, and our conflicts; anger is a sin, and is one of the deadly sins that Christ's precious blood cleansed from all believers the moment they gave their life to him. The cure and remedy for human anger is total surrender to the Lordship of Jesus Christ. Anger makes people live fearful, unsafe, insecure, untrusting, and shameful lives that occupy human hearts. But the love of God in Christ Jesus our Lord and the help of the Holy Spirit will cleanse all our anger and rage that leads to destructive lives.

    Christian believers must surrender their

God Where Are You?

anger to the hands of Jesus Christ in order to live a peaceful life from this earth to heaven.

Chapter 7: Where is God In Time of Immoralities?

Sexual immorality is an abomination to the Lord God. If any man or woman were forced to lie with each other, they were guilty of sin. Similarly, the gospel of Mathew tells us that whoever looked at a woman to lust after her has already committed adultery with her in his heart. Paul revealed: "Everything is permissible for me, but not everything is beneficial.

Everything is permissible for me, but I will be mastered by anything. Food for the stomach and the stomach for food, but God will destroy them both. The body is not meant for sexual immorality, but for the Lord, and the Lord for the body" (1st Corinthian 12:20). By his power, God raised the Lord from the dead, and he will raise us also. Do you not know that your bodies are members of Christ himself? Shall I then take the members of Christ and unite them with a prostitute? Do you not know that he who unites himself with a prostitute is one with her in body? For it is said that the two will become one flesh. But he who unites himself with the Lord is one with him in spirit. Flee from sexual immorality. All other sins a man commits are outside his body, but he who sins sexually sins against his own body. Do you not know that your body is a temple of the Holy Spirit, who is in you, whom you have received from God? You are not your own; you were bought at a price.

Therefore, honor God with your body" (1st Corinthian 6:12-20). This Scripture clearly explains Apostle Paul's argument with the Corinthian believers and with us today concerning Christian believers' freedom in Christ. They thought they had the freedom to do anything they wanted to do, but Paul made it clear to them, as well as he taught them in his teaching, that there are things that Christian believers were not permissible to do as members of Jesus Christ. Apostle Paul, in his teaching, warns us against moral loyalty and lets us know the terrible consequences of sexual immorality for the believers. When a believer joins his body to an immoral man or woman, it causes him to become one with him or her, to come under her domination to desecrate what the cross has made holy and to save himself from the Kingdom of God the Father almighty. In sexual immorality, people virtually remove themselves from union with Christ by making their bodies members of immoral and ungodly persons. All the believing Christians are urging to flee from sexual immorality lifestyle; sexual morality is particularly abhorrent to the Lord God. More than any other sinful act, it desecrates the body; it devalues the body, which is the temple of the Holy Spirit that lives in us. Therefore, Apostle Paul gave the admonition and cried out to all the believers then and to us today to flee and run from sexual immorality lifestyle.

Believing Christians must make all efforts repeatedly to run away, to be strong enough to make themselves say no to all forms of sexual immorality and all ungodliness and worldly passions. The children of God must live self-control, be upright, and live godly lives in this world; this is God's desire for all his children. Moreover, all the believing Christians on his earth must know that their body is the personal dwelling place of the Holy Spirit, where the Spirit of God's mark is placed on us that belongs to him. For those who totally gave their life to Jesus Christ truthfully and faithfully, the Holy Spirit lives the life of Jesus Christ through us. Our body, spirit, and soul belong to God; our body must never be defiled by any impurity or evil, whether by immoral thoughts, desires, deeds, films, booking magazines, or the internet. Believers must live in such a way as to honor and please God with our bodies. Sexual immorality is a sin against God, who created us in his own image and gave us his holy spirit. The Scripture revealed: "In you, one man commits a detestable offense with his neighbor's wife, another shamefully defiles his daughter-in-law, and another violates his sister, his own father's daughter. For they have committed adultery, and blood is on their hands.

They committed adultery with their idols; they even sacrificed their children, whom they bore to me, as food for them. They have also done this to me; at that same time, they defiled my sanctuary and desecrated my Sabbaths. On the very day, they sacrificed their children to their idols, they entered my statuary and desecrated it; that is what they did in my house" (Ezekiel 22:11; 23:37-39). During this time of Prophet Ezekiel, Jerusalem had become a city of violence and all forms of wickedness. There was no longer any respect for the things of God and all holy things; family, the poor, and the needy made sexual immorality rampant as well as cheating, bribery, and stealing were happening in every commonplace.

All this happened because the people had turned away from God and from his word and commandment. Therefore, God was giving the city over to severe judgment and destruction. In the same way, today, the social and spiritual condition of cities throughout the world is similar to ancient Jerusalem.

Unless the people of this world repent in

all the cities and towns, they will be punished and perish with their sins, just as the people in Jerusalem in the Old Testament time.

Nations, cities, towns, and people in this world cannot despise God's order, His word, and his commandments, as well as his ways for humanity without the ultimate in reaping and facing the consequences. Sexual immorality is a grace sin in the sight of God. Our Lord Jesus Christ, during his earthly ministry, teaches: "But I tell you that anyone who divorces his wife, except for marital unfaithfulness, causes her to become an adulteress, and anyone who marries the divorced woman commits adultery. I tell you that anyone who divorces his wife, except for marital unfaithfulness, and marries another woman commits adultery" (Matthew 5:32; 19:9)

God disapproved of marital unfaithfulness in marriage: God's plan and standard for marriage is one man and one woman joined together for life and to be dissolved only when death does their part. Our Lord Jesus Christ gives an exception, namely marital unfaithfulness. Marital unfaithfulness includes any adultery or sexual immorality; therefore, divorce is to be permitted when sexual immorality is involved.

The Biblical facts concerning divorce that Jesus Christ is not criticizing is the separation because of adultery, but a divorce permitted in the Old Testament in those days when a husband could discover premarital unchastity after the marriage ceremony had taken place. God's desire in such cases was that the two remain together. However, he permitted divorce due to premarital unchastity because of the hardness of the people of Israel's hearts. In the case of immorality after marriage, the Old Testament Law prescribed the dissolving of the marriage by executing both the offending parties; this, of course, will leave the innocent one free to remarry. Under the new covenant, the privileges of the believer are no less. Although divorce is a tragedy to the children in the marriage, marital unfaithfulness is such a cruel sin against one's spouse that Jesus Christ states that the innocent party has a proper right to end the marriage by divorce in order that they can be free to remarry another Christian believer. Apostle Paul's treatment of marriage goes further if it ends in desertion; he indicates that marriage also may be dissolved if it is the desertion of an unbelieving Christian spouse. Paul further shows that remarrying by the believer in such cases is not a sin. Sexual immorality is not approved in any marriage; it does not show love for one another, and it can cause incurable diseases that might lead to death, such as HIV, AIDs, and all other diseases that the other party might contaminate other people.

Adultery is a sin in the sight of God. All Christian believers must make all efforts to live a pure and clean life. Believers must deny any physical and spiritual lust after other women or men after false gods or idols; they must conduct their behavior at a high moral standard and at a high spiritual level. Sexual activities must be in a marriage relationship only. Sexual immorality is composed of adultery, prostitution, sexual relationships between unmarried individuals, homosexuality, and fornication; sensuality is unholy, unnatural, and impure sexual activity. Adultery destroys marriage and devalues the adulterer. The Scripture revealed: "I am afraid that when I come again my God will humble me before you, and I will be grieved over many who have sinned earlier and have not repented of the impurity, sexual sin and debauchery in which they have indulged" (2nd Corinthian 12:21) Apostle Paul was dealing with the immorality and sexual sin that was going on in the Corinthian Church during his missionary journey there; he was very grieved over immoralities that was ruling the life of those within the church who are quarreling, jealous, angry, divisive, slandering, gossiping, arrogant and wrath all forms of disorderly conduct. Paul's grief is a grief to God and a reproach to the name of Jesus Christ. The prospect of having to deal with these kinds of sins, as well as individuals who were unrepentant of impurity, sexual sin, and debauchery, was a great grief to the spirit of God, Christ, that dwells in Paul as well. In some churches today, the same activities are going on among the Christians, whereby they think that they can pray for forgiveness and it will be Okay.

In the Book of Colossians, the Scripture revealed: "Put to death, therefore, whatever belongs to your earthly nature: sexual immorality, impurity, lust, evil desires, and greed, which is idolatry. Because of these, the wrath of God is coming. You used to walk in these ways in the life you once lived. But now you must rid yourselves of all such things as these: anger, rage, malice, slander, and filth language from your lips. Do not lie to each other, since you have taken off your old self with its practices and have put on the new self, which is being renewed in knowledge in the image of its creator" (Colossians 3:5-10) All the believing Christians must get rid of greed, which is idolatry among other things it is allowing material things to become the focus of a person's desires and value.

Money replaces Jesus Christ as our master, and things displace reliance on and daily faith in God himself. For this reason, greed is idolatry; believers must stay clear of it in any of their daily lives. "Marriage should be honored by all, and the marriage bed kept pure, for God will judge the adulterer and all the sexually immoral" (Hebrews 13:4). All the Christian believers that are called in Jesus Christ to be morally and sexually pure means to refraining from all the activities and thoughts that incite desire not in accordance with one's virginity before marriage or one's marriage covenant after marriage. Believers must restraint and avoid all sexual stimulation to activity that could defile their purity before God almighty. Believers must be able to control their own bodies with the power of the Holy Spirit in a way that is Holy and honorable and in any passionate lust. God the Father, Son, and Holy Spirit, one God, forever has high standards for his people in marriage and sexuality. For God loves those who live righteously according to his commandments.

God Where Are You?

Chapter 8: Where is God In Time of Imprisonment?

All Christian believers must remember and pray for those who are in prison all over the world, especially for all the persecuting Christians who are in prison because of their faith and because they were there because they were sharing the good news of Jesus Christ to the sinners. The scripture revealed: "The Spirit of the Sovereign Lord is on me because the Lord has anointed me to preach good news to the poor. He has sent me to bind up the brokenhearted, to proclaim freedom for the captives and release from darkness for the prisoners, to proclaim the year of the Lord's favor and the day of vengeance of our God. To comfort all who mourn, and provide for those who grieve in Zion to bestow on them a crown of beauty instead of ashes, the oil of gladness instead of mourning and a garment of praise instead of a spirit of despair" (Isaiah 61:1-3) This verse of the scripture; our Lord Jesus Christ in the Synagogue during his earthly ministry. The Spirit of the Messiah and his anointing relate to our Lord Jesus Christ, who is the only Messiah, his mission, and his ministry on earth. Prophet Isaiah gave a clear, direct description of the spiritual character and stature of the Messiah. When Jesus Christ began his earthly ministry, he quoted and applied these scripture to himself. In order to fulfill his ministry, Jesus was anointed with the Holy Spirit. His anointed ministry involved preaching the gospel to the poor, the meek, and the afflicted; healing and binding up the spiritual and physically sick and broken-hearted; breaking the bonds of evil and proclaiming freedom from sin and Satanic dominion and opening the spiritual eyes of the lost that they might see the light of the gospel and be saved. This fourfold purpose characterized Jesus Christ's entire ministry, and it will continue to be fulfilled by the church as long as it is on the earth. The Lord Jesus Christ anointed them to open the gate of prisons on earth and release them from the domain of darkness into his marvelous light. The favor includes the ideas of good pleasure acceptance, blessing, and desires of hearts; this is the salvation of our Lord and they ear of God's redemption, which Jesus Christ applied to himself during his earthly ministry, which lasted for three and half years before he was crucified.

Believing Christians must make all efforts to help the prisoners in this world's nations. The scripture revealed: "Remember those in prison as if you were their fellow prisoners and those who are mistreated as if you yourselves were suffering. So we say with confidence. The Lord is my helper; I will not be afraid. What can man do to me?" (Hebrews 13:3, 6) believers in Christ must help all the persecuting Christians who are in prison in all the nations. We pray to Christ, who is the head of the church, the cornerstone of the church;

the Lord is our helper no matter how limited our earthly possessions may be or how trying our circumstances are; we never need to fear that maybe God will not desert or forsake us. Our heavenly Father cares for us. Therefore, we can say with confidence and boldness that the Lord is our helper; he is the helper of those in prison.

This can be affirmed with confidence in times of distress, trials, or trouble in prison and anywhere we may be on this earth.

Many people who are in prison for injustice, especially the persecuted Christians, sometimes ask the same question: where are you, Lord? Deliver me from the hands of the wicked. The scripture revealed when Paul was in prison and continually praying to the Lord, The Lord answered and said: "Three times I pleaded with the Lord to take it away from me. But he said to me, "My grace is sufficient for you, for my power is made perfect in weakness; therefore, I will boast all the more gladly about my weaknesses so that Christ's power may rest one. (2nd Corinthian 12: 8-9) Jesus says that even if his followers face tough times and get thrown into prison because they're doing what's right, God's grace and support will help them get through it. It means that God's help is like a strong power that gives them the strength to handle the difficulties that come with being in prison or facing persecution. Jesus wants his followers to know that they're not alone in these challenges, and with God's grace, they can face and overcome challenging situations while staying true to what's right. God almighty's grace and power are most clearly seen and profoundly revealed in the midst of our human weaknesses. The greater our suffering, weakness, trials, and persecution for Jesus Christ, the more God's grace will be given to accomplish his will. What our Lord and Savior give is always sufficient for us to live our daily lives, to work for him, and to endure our suffering and any obstacles we might be going through; as long as we draw near to Jesus Christ, Christ Jesus will give us his heavenly strength and his comfort. We Christian believers should boast and see the eternal value in our weaknesses because they cause Christ's power to rest on us and live within us as we walk through life toward our heavenly home.

In the Holy scripture, we read: "The poor will see and be glad – you who seek God, may your heart live! The Lord hears the needy and does not despise his captive people" (Psalm 69:32-33). The Lord, in his mercy, hears the cries of the poor and the needy, and also he hears the prayers of those who are in prison, captive of imprisonment in all the nations; some of them are there for what they did not do. The Lord God almighty Father said: "See, I have engraved you on the palms, of my hands; your walls are ever before me" (Isaiah 49:16) The Lord has never forsaken those who are in prisons in all the nations in this world and God's words of assurance are for all his believing children who are being persecuted for righteousness and those who are going through trying times, all diverse difficulties.

God the Father's love for us and the prisoners is greater than the natural affection of a loving mother for her children; it is, therefore, unthinkable that he will ever forget us, especially in our times of despair and grief. His compassion for the prisoners and the captives will never be delayed, regardless of life's circumstances; he watches over them with great tenderness and love, and they may rest in the conviction that he will never leave them. The evidence of God's great love is that he has engraved the prisoners on the palms of his own hands so that he can never forget them; the scars on his hands are always before his eyes as a reminder of the great love he has showered on all the captives and the prisoners and of his desire as to take care of them. The truth will prevail, and the captive, the prison, will be set free. The scripture revealed: "Remember those who are in prison as if you were their fellow prisoners, and those who are mistreated as if you yourselves were suffering (Hebrews 13:3). Christian brotherhood comes from our mutual relationship with the Father and his Son. As we participate in the grace of Jesus Christ, we are all made sons and daughters with him and fellow heirs of the Father's blessings; because of this brotherhood, we are taught by the Father almighty to love each other no matter what condition they may be, and whatever they are going through. Jesus Christ's commandments entail much more than doing this, such as visiting prisons and hospitals, helping those who are in need of help, or avoiding others. All Christians who believe in Jesus should follow his commandments by adopting his way of life, marked by genuine concern and care for others. Christ's commandments are the most self-engaging and challenging of all! It is comforting when Christ Jesus says, "I will not leave you as orphans. No, we are not orphans because the spirit of the risen Jesus comes to abide in us, which is the spirit of truth. Let mourn with those who mourn and rejoice with those who are rejoicing; pray for those who are in prison, especially all the persecuting Christians all over the world. Let us live a sacrificial life for Jesus Christ, one and only, who came down from heaven and gave his life for us so that those of us who live do not live for ourselves but for him who gave his life for us, so that we may live with him forever in heaven.

The scripture revealed: "may the groans of the prisoners come before you; by the strength of your arm preserve, those condemned to die" (Psalm 79:11). God holds the prisoners in his arm, and he strengthens them from day to day, especially all the persecuting Christians. We also have the revealing scripture: Let this be written for future generations, that a people not yet created may praise the Lord; The Lord looked down from his sanctuary on high, from heaven he viewed the earth, to hear the groans of the prisoners and release those condemned to death. So the name of the Lord will be declared in Zion and his praise in Jerusalem" (Psalm 102:18-21). In any circumstances, in times of trouble, great distress in life, when everything seems to be going wrong, and we find ourselves helpless to change the situation that imprisons us, our only hope is to call on our

God almighty Father and place our lives and our troubles and circumstances in his holy hands.

Prisoners, captives, and persecuting Christians must cry out to the Lord for mercy and ask for his divine intervention.

They must be confident that the Lord will answer their prayers and he will not forsake them. The scripture revealed and made it clear: "Humble yourselves, therefore, under God's mighty hand, that he may lift you up in due time. Cast all your anxiety on him because he cares for you" (1st Peter 5:6-7). God did not forget those who are in prisons on all the earth; they are his children. He cares for the troubles of every one of his children, a truth emphasized throughout his words. All their fears, anxieties, and concerns must be decisively given to our Lord and Savior, Jesus Christ care, who says: "I am in prison. You did not visit me, and we said, Lord, when are you in prison that we did not visit you? And the Lord said, if you did not do it for any of my brothers and sisters in the world, you did not do it for me." We must pray for those who are in prisons all over the nations, persecuted for their faith in Jesus Christ, as well as those who are in jail for injustice. We must pray for the truth to prevail and for the persecuted Christian prisoners to be released to continue their service of the work of the Lord.

Chapter 9: Where Is God In Time Of Sickness & Diseases

Many people in this world wonder and ask questions such as where is God when they have diseases of Cancer, sickle cell, diabetes, Eczema, and all kinds of diverse diseases.

When people distance themselves from God, the Almighty Father, they often find themselves involved in various unhealthy lifestyles, starting with their dietary choices and extending to a range of immoral activities.

This creates an opening for the enemy, Satan, the author of all evil, to take control of their lives. In this state, they may neglect to spend time reading the word of God, which has the power to cleanse them from anything that can contaminate their spirit, soul, and body. God's word serves as a preventive measure, cleansing them from potential diseases before they occur, and trusting in the Lord allows Him to take care of these concerns for them. They are not paying, crying unto God, the one and holy who hears prayers and answers our prayers to send his word from heaven and heal them.

The scripture revealed: "The righteous cry out, and the Lord hears them, and he delivers them from all their troubles. The Lord is close to the brokenhearted and saves those who are crushed in spirit. A righteous man may have many troubles, but the Lord delivers him from them all; he protects all his bones, not one of them will be broken" (Psalm 34:20). God almighty from the Old Testament to the New Testament promised blessing of healthy life and prosperity for those who obeyed his words and his law. Get, alongside his promise, is the reality that the righteous may have many troubles, afflictions, persecutions, illnesses, sicknesses, and diseases because of their belief in God. Living a righteous life will not necessarily keep them from trouble and suffering in this life. On the contrary, commitment to God, the Holy Trinity, often brings testing and persecution. God Almighty has ordained that we must endure many hardships to enter his Kingdom. The suffering of the righteous must be counterbalanced by the revelation that the Lord God almighty wishes to deliver us out of all our diseases and troubles. When the purpose of permitting affliction is accomplished, Jesus Christ will then deliver us from them either by direct supernatural intervention in this life or by victorious death and transference to the life hereafter. There are no diseases of the righteous that God the Father, Son, and God the Holy Spirit cannot heal. We also read in another scripture that says: "Apostle Paul was going through diseases called" A thorn in my flesh; a messenger of Satan, to torment me> Three times I pleaded with the Lord to take it away from me. But he said to me, my grace is sufficient for you, for my power is made perfect in weakness. Therefore, I will boast all the more gladly about my weaknesses so that Christ's power may rest on me (2nd Corinthians 12: 7b-9). During the time that apostle Paul was going through the illness of a thorn in the flesh, he did not do anything other than just call on the Lord for his healing. The Lord answered his prayer by letting him know that his race was all-sufficient for him. Grace is God's presence, favor, and power. God's grace and power are most clearly seen and profoundly revealed in the midst of our human weaknesses. The greater our weaknesses and trials for Jesus Christ, the more the grace of God will give us to accomplish his will in our lives. What Christ gives is always sufficient for us to live our daily lives, work for him, and endure our suffering and diseases of thorns that might afflict our body and flesh. As long as we are drawn near the Lord Jesus Christ, the great physician, Christ will give us his heavenly strength and comfort. We should boast and see eternal value in our weaknesses, for they cause Jesus Christ's power to rest on us and live within us as we walk through life toward our heavenly home. The scripture revealed in the gospel of Mathew is: "When evening comes, many who were demon-possessed were brought to him, and he drove out the spirits with a word and healed all the sick. This was to fulfill what was spoken through the prophet Isaiah: "He took up our infirmities and carried our diseases" (Mathew 8:16-17)

The problem of sickness and disease is intertwined with the issue of sin and death, which are the consequences of the fall in the

Garden of Eden. The medical sciences might view the causes of sickness and diseases in different ways, such as physiological or psychosomatic terms. In contrast, the Holy scripture presents them as spiritual causes, as the underlying or as a fundamental problem of sin that contaminates and affects our spiritual and physical flesh. God's provision in his redemptive work is as extensive as the consequences of sin which came after the fall. God provides forgiveness for our sins and for death; God provides eternal and resurrection life; for the sickness and diseases, God almighty provides healing during the time of our Lord Jesus Christ's earthly ministry, his threefold ministry was: One - teaching the word of God, Two - Preaching the gospel of repentance which is the sin problem. Three –

The blessings of the Kingdom of God, which is life in him, healing all diverse sicknesses, diseases, and forms of infirmity that plaque all the people of his days. The will of God concerning healing is revealed in the Holy scripture – God promised good health and healing for his people on this earth if they remained faithful to his commandments. God promised that he would never bring diseases as a judgment to his people - He said: "I am the Lord, who heals you as redeemer." God almighty continues to be our great physician, our doctor, and the healer of his people from the Old Testament to the New Testament. When people call unto him in their sickness and diseases, seek his face diligently, and obey his word, he will touch them, send his word from heaven, and heal them. Jesus Christ, the one and only the incarnate Son of God, was and is the exact representation of God's nature and character. Jesus Christ is the revealer of God's Willing action; he shows conclusively that it is in God's heart, in his nature, and in his purpose to heal all who are sick and those who are possessed and oppressed by the devil. Although Jesus Christ did not heal every ill person during his earthly ministry, the gospel revealed that he healed all those who came to him, individually and in groups like the ten lepers; he healed those who were brought to him time. He asked them if they believed that he could heal them, and if they said yes, they were instantly healed. An example is the man who has been suffering for thirty-eight years sitting at the pool of Bethsaida. Healing was a regular part of our Lord Jesus Christ's proclamation of the Kingdom of God.

Up till today, those who believe in Jesus Christ's power of healing when they call out to him, he sends his word from the right hand of God where he sat and healed them. Sometimes, unconfessed sin hinders our prayer of healing, and failure to pray faithfully also hinders the answer to our prayer of healing. People who are sick and suffering from any form of disease must surrender their lives faithfully to Jesus Christ with a strong faith in him in order to be able to receive his power of healing.

The scripture revealed: "But I will restore you to health and heal your wounds, declares the Lord because you are called an outcast; Zion for whom no one cares" (Jeremiah 30:17). Jesus Christ our Lord has intimate access to God; therefore, he will have a priestly ministry, which will result in the nations' restoration to their spiritual vitality and worship that God the Father had always intended from his people. "Nevertheless, I will bring health and healing to it; I will heal my people and will let them enjoy abundant peace and security" (Jeremiah 33:6). People of this earth will receive abundant peace when their diseases and sickness are taken care of by Jesus Christ. Compare this to the false prophets who had been proclaiming a false peace.

Prophet Jeremiah offered the word of assurance and hope of true peace in the Lord. The word "Peace" Is far more than the absence of war, conflict, or stress; it means the positive presence of harmony, wholeness, soundness, well-being, and success in all areas of our lives. Peace can be when people are free from all their diseases and sicknesses.

It can be experienced as wholeness and harmonious relationships both inside the home; it can also refer to the settlement of war between nations or within nations, as during times of prosperity and civil war. It can also refer to one's personal sense of wholeness and well-being, from fear and tribulation, at peace within one's own spirit, soul, and body, and with God. We have to know that when God created the heavens and the earth, he created a world at peace. When Adam and Eve sinned by listening to the voice of Satan and ate from the forbidden tree, their disobedience introduced sin and disrupted creation's original harmony. At that moment, Adam and Eve's sin made them experience, for the first time, guilt and shame before God and brought a loss to their inner peace. The scripture revealed: "But he was pierced for our transgressions, he was crushed for our iniquities; the punishment that brought us peace was upon him, and by his wounds, we are healed" (Isaiah 53:5) by our Lord Jesus Christ's wounds on the day of his crucifixion we are healed. Christ's healing refers to our salvation with all its benefits, both spiritual and physical. Sickness and disease are the result of the fall and Satan's activity in the world.

The reason why Jesus Christ came to the world was to destroy the work of the devil. Jesus Christ gave the gift of healing to the church. He commanded those who belonged to him to heal the sick and cast out demons and diseases as part of their proclamation of God's

Kingdom on this earth. The Holy Spirit gave all the believing Christians the power of healing as part of the great commission of Jesus Christ, who said: "God ye into all the nations baptizing them in the name of the Father, Son, and Holy Spirit, healing the sick, preach the gospel to the people of the world, shelter the homeless help those who are in need; but not all the Christians carry out this commandment in full, some are very scared to pray for the sick, or those who are in the hospital. The scripture revealed: "News about him spread all over Syria, and people brought to him all who were ill with various diseases, those suffering severe pain, the demon-possessed those having seizures, and the paralyzed, and he healed them." (Matthew 4:24) The scripture states clearly that the gospel of God's Kingdom is with healing, the performing of the miracles of divine healing, and the driving out of demons from those who are demon-possessed. The Kingdom includes blessings for the spirit, soul, and body. Jesus Christ commissioned his twelve disciples and us today to heal the sick as part of our assignment of the proclamation of the Kingdom of God. Christian churches all over the world must take the healing ministry as part of the preaching of the gospel. God's healing power and faith were imparted through the church (1) Laying on of hands by praying for the sick, (2) confession of known and unknown sin by those who are sick with oil, and the prayer of faith, (3) spiritual gifts of healing are given to the church the elders of the church must pray the prayer of faith. Some churches fail to seek and obtain the gifts of miracles and healing as God intended them to do. Unbelief can also hinder the prayer of the sick. Self-centeredness and self-righteous behavior can also hinder the prayer of the sick. The scripture revealed: "Dear friend, I pray that you may enjoy good health and that all may go well with you, even as your soul is getting along well" (3rd John 1:2). It is God's provision and intention that we as believers of Jesus Christ be healthy and his blessings accompany our lives. He wants all to go well with us on our work, plan, and purposes, our ministry, our families, and everything we do to go according to God's will and his direction. Therefore, God's blessings through redemption in Jesus Christ are intended to meet both physical and spiritual needs. The scripture revealed: "Is anyone of you sick? He should call the church elders to pray over him and anoint him with oil in the name of the Lord. And the prayer offered in faith will make the sick person well. The Lord will raise him up if he has sinned, he will be forgiven.

Therefore, confess your sins to each other and pray for each other so that you may be healed. The prayer of a righteous man is powerful and effective" (James 5:14-16). We may deal with physical, mental, or emotional illness by asking for the prayers of the elders or leaders of the church. Pastors and leaders of the church are to pray for the sick and to anoint them with oil. It is the elder's responsibility to pray the prayer of faith and not the responsibility of the sick person. The New Testament placed the significant burden for the healing of the sick on the church and its leaders. The anointing of the oil represents the healing power of the Holy Spirit. It is used as an aid or booster of faith. It is the prayer that Apostle James emphasizes as most important. Effective prayer must be offered in faith if the sick are to be healed.

The Lord Jesus Christ will give faith according to his will. Some diseases may not always be healed automatically and instantly; nevertheless, the church must continue to pray to seek the healing power of the Holy Spirit for those who are sick and ill and to the glory of Jesus Christ, our Lord, the great healer. Apostle James also recognizes that some sicknesses may be due to sin; therefore, the people of this world, especially the believers, should examine themselves before the Lord in prayer to know if the disease or sickness is due to personal sin.

If this is the case, sin must be confessed to others, and fervent prayer for one another must be made to God. Sin in the church hinders the prayers of the believers and can block God's healing power from being manifested in the congregation. The prayers of good and faithful people draw them closer to God. These prayers open the door to a life filled with the Holy Spirit, giving strength for serving others and growing in their faith. Praying also helps them understand what Jesus has provided for them and empowers them to overcome challenges.

In addition, these prayers create a strong connection with God, bringing His grace, mercy, and peace. They lead others to Jesus and provide wisdom and knowledge about

Him. These prayers bring healing, rescue from problems, and give thanks to God, making the presence of Jesus very real. Most importantly, they assure believers of their final salvation and remind them that Jesus is always there for them. James 5:16: "The prayer of a righteous man is powerful and effective." The scripture revealed: "Praise the Lord, O my soul, and forget not all his benefits – who forgives all your sins and heals all your disease" (Psalm 103:2-3). We people of this world must give praises to God, thankfulness, and praise to the Lord for all the benefits that he bestows on all the believing covenant people. We must never forget the goodness of God to us, his children.

We must be thankful for the blessings showered on us through the power of the Holy Spirit. It is the human race that experiences sin, sickness, and death. God's blessings of forgiveness of sins bring healing for our diseases and the gift of eternal life. Forgiveness is the first and most important gift we can receive from God. Healing of diseases that come to us because of sin, and Satan makes God's salvation available to his people who gave their life to him. The scripture revealed: "Come, let us return to the Lord. He has torn us to pieces, but he will heal us; he has injured us, but he will bind up our wounds" (Hosea 6:1). God almighty Father calls us to repentance., of assurance that though God must judge sin, he always desires to heal us and restore us then and now and forever. God almighty heals diseases and sicknesses through prayer. "Go back and tell Hezekiah, the leader of my people, this is what the Lord, the God of your father David, says: I have heard your prayers and seen your tears: I will heal you. On the third day from now, you will defend this city and go up to the temple of the Lord. I will add fifteen years to your life. And I will deliver you and this city from the hand of the King of Assyria. I will defend this city for my sake and for the sake of my servant David" (2nd King 20:5-6). God, the Father almighty, is a delivered and healer of all diseases and sicknesses; he has the power to decrease our age or increase our age for his own glory. The scripture revealed: "When he heard this Jesus said, "When he heard this, Jesus said, "This sickness will not end in death. No, it is for God's glory so that God's Son may be glorified through it." (John 11:4). Up till today believers' diseases, sicknesses and illness is for the glory of God as well as all the believer's afflictions, and trouble are for the glory of God the Father, the Son and God the Holy spirit.

Sickness among God's people will never result in death as the final outcome. The power of the resurrection has destroyed death. Christ Jesus destroyed the power of sin and death on the Cross. All believers live for the glory of God, either in sickness or in health. The final truth is that those who believe in Jesus Christ will never die; when we suffer or are sick, it does not mean that Jesus Christ doesn't love us. It means Christ wanted to make things new in our lives, spirit, soul, and body.

Children of God must always know that God is always with us. Christ delayed when they told him Lazarus was sick, but he had made him alive. At that very moment, when he got to Mary and Martha's house, he called Lazarus out of the grave—blessed him with a new life. Jesus Christ said that his delay is not for lack of love, mercy, or compassion. Still, it is for the glory of God, for the manifestation proclamation of God's Kingdom, and for the ultimate eternal good of those who are suffering. Our confidence must not be based on, rest on, or depend on what God is presently doing but on who God is in our lives: a caring, loving Savior of the people of the world.

Chapter 10: Where Is God In Time of War & Difficulties of Life?

Where is God during times of war, rumors of war between nations, and civil war within the nation, and during all life's difficulties, people are asking? People of the world stay away from God; they don't want to hear his name, and they don't want to listen to his word. But when life's afflictions come, such as civil war or war between the nations, or difficulties, such as loss of jobs or loved ones.

People will start screaming at God and calling on his name; they will want to know why he allows bad things to happen to them. The scripture revealed: "Be strong and courageous. Do not be afraid or terrified because of the, for the Lord your God goes with you; he will never leave you nor forsake you. Then Moses summoned Joshua and said to him in the presence of all Israel, be strong and courageous, for you must go with this people into the land that the Lord swore to their inheritance. The Lord himself goes before you and will be with you; he will never leave you nor forsake you. Do not be afraid; do not be discouraged." (Deuteronomy 1:6-8)

The promises of God are from the Old Testament to the New Testament to all who sincerely and faithfully give their life to Jesus Christ as Lord and as their Savior. Believers are assured that if they love God above all else and solely wholeheartedly depend on him rather than on material security, the Lord will never desert nor forsake them but will be their helper in times of wars, rumors of wars, and in all earthly difficulties. Because of this promise, we must be strong and courageous; persevering in all forms of worldly trials and afflictions, believers must resist temptations, trust in the Lord, and entirely faithfully and sincerely obey his words and commandments.

In another scripture, we read: "David also said to Solomon his son, be strong and courageous, and do the work do not be afraid or discouraged for the Lord God, my God, is with you. He will not fail you or forsake you until all the work for the service of the temple of the Lord is finished" (1st Chronicles 28:20). David's charge to his son Solomon was that he must seek to have the knowledge of God at all times; to serve the Lord and seek his face wholehearted, with a willing mind.

To have the knowledge of God in our lives is to maintain a close relationship with the Lord and live in his word always, desire his grace and mercy in everything we are doing and about to do in our businesses in the ministry of the church. We must strive to receive the Kingdom's power and righteousness to such an extent that we continually pray for his active presence in our lives and earnestly seek to obey his will, hungry and thirsty for righteousness.

Scripture revealed: "When you go into

battle in your own land against an enemy who is oppressing you, sound a blast on the trumpets. Then you will be remembered by the Lord your God and rescued from your enemies" (Number 10:9) in any battle Go almighty Father will remind us what he has done for us in the past so that we are not afraid. God always helped his children in war, on the battlefield, only if he was called, summoned by the sound of the trumpets. In other words, God placed certain conditions on the children of Israel for receiving his help. God may not move on our behalf if we refuse to draw near to him in prayer and supplication, crying out for his grace, mercy, protection, and presence. In another scripture concerning war: "Moses answered the people, do not be afraid of them. Stand firm, and you will see the deliverance the

Lord will bring you today.

The Egyptians you see today you will never see again. The Lord will fight for you; you need only to be still" (Exodus 14:13-14). God the Father almighty always gives us the word of assurance. In the Old Testament, he assured the people of Israel that he would fight for them, but they had to move forward toward the sea in faith. God fought for his people as they walked in faith and in obedience to his word then and the same today. We also have the Lord's words of assurance in the holy scripture: "The Lord is my shepherd; I shall not be in want....... (Psalm 23:1-6) From the Old Testament to the New Testament, he is our shepherd. God almighty compares himself to a shepherd in order to illustrate his great love for his people. Our Lord Jesus Christ himself told us the same thing during his earthly ministry.

The Lord expresses his relationship to those who believe in him, those who gave their life to him. He said: "I am the good shepherd. The good shepherd lays down his life for the sheep; I am the good shepherd I know my sheep and my sheep know me just as the Father knows me and I know the Father, and I lay down my life for the sheep" 11,14-15) Our Lord said: "I tell you the truth, I am the gate for the sheep. All who ever came before me were thieves and robbers, but the sheep did not listen to them. I am the gate; whoever enters through me will be saved" (7-9). Our Lord Jesus Christ is the shepherd of his people. There are no earthly difficulties that he cannot handle for us. God the Father, through Jesus Christ and by the power of the Holy Spirit, is so concerned about every individual of his children that he desires to love, care for us, protect us, guide us, and be near to us, just as a good shepherd does for his own sheep. All the Christian believers are the Lord Jesus Christ's sheep. We belong to him and are the special objects of his affection and attention. The book of the prophet Isaiah says: "We all like sheep have gone astray" (Isaiah 53:6). The Lord has redeemed us with his precious blood shed on the Calvary tree, and we now forever belong to him. As his sheep, we can claim his promises and his power when we allow him with a sincere heart.

We will not lack anything necessary for God's almighty Father's will and will be accomplished in our life in so much that we will be content in the good shepherd's provision during any earthly difficulties and trouble and war, even in time of personal hardship, because I trust in his love and his commandment to us. Because of his nearness and his full presence, we are free from fears. The Holy Spirit is our counselor, helper, paraclete heavenly guest, and communicator who brings Jesus Christ's message to us and the presence of Jesus Christ to our hearts. Our confidence rests in his presence, Jesus, and the word of God; we are necessary for an abundant life. Christ Jesus always leads us during our earthly troubles, difficulties, and afflictions, leading us to a still water by the power of the Holy Spirit. Whenever we face discouragement or rejection, the good shepherd always revives us and re-energizes our souls through his power and grace. He guides us to the way of holiness, as we are obedient to his words. In times of danger, difficulties, and even death, we fear no evil because we know that Christ Jesus is always with us in every situation of life; his power and authority never fail on all those who believe in him. God's rod and staff, weapon of defense or discipline, which symbolizes his strength in our lives, all reassure us of the Lord's love, mercy, and guidance in our lives.

The Lord God almighty cares for all our needs in the middle of the evil forces that attempt to destroy our lives and our souls. God provided us with sufficient grace to live a life of rejoicing in the Lord's presence so that we may be able to eat at the table that he set for us. Full of praises, thankfulness, and hope, and full of peace and protected by his precious shed blood and broken body. The Lord anointed his people with oil, which means special favor, and pours his blessings through the power of the Holy Spirit to the point that only his goodness and mercy will follow us through our life's pilgrimage on earth; we will constantly receiving his love, grace, help, kindness and heavenly support no matter what happens to us, or what we are going through we will always trust that the Lord the Good shepherd will work in all things for my good, and for his glory. We may be able to live with him from this earth to heaven.

In another scripture, we read: "You will hear of wars and rumors of wars, but see to it that you are not alarmed. Such things must happen, but the end is still to come. Nation will rise against nation and Kingdom against

Kingdom.

There will be famines and earthquakes in various places. All these are the beginning of birth pains. Then you will be handed over to be persecuted and put to death, and you will be hated by all nations because of me" (Matthew 24:6-9). Our Lord Jesus Christ warned us about what is going to happen before his return, his second coming to earth, to judge the dead and the living, and to set up his Kingdom of righteousness and peace on earth. All believing Christians may expect troubles, tribulations, and persecutions, such as Islamic State-ISIS slaughtering Christians in the church on Palm Sunday during our life's pilgrimage on earth.

Suffering for Christ because of our loyalty to him and his word, which is an intrinsic part of the Christian faith.

Christians must also be very careful because of false prophets, false teachers, and preachers who are making millions by using the name of the Lord, even though they do not know him. In the book of James, the scripture revealed:

"My dear brothers, take note of this; everyone should be quick to listen, slow to speak, and slow to become angry, for man's anger does not bring about the righteous life that God desires.

Therefore, get rid of all moral filth and the evil that is so prevalent and humbly accept the word planted in you, which can save you" (James 1:19-21). All the believing Christians must take this scripture verse seriously. Christians must get rid of all moral filth. The word of God, either preached or written, cannot effectively take hold of a person's life if they are not separated from the moral filth and evil in the world. In order for Christians to stay out of earthly troubles and difficulties, they must follow the commandments of God; as believers, they must set aside all the ungodly lust and filth that permeates our corrupt society that seeks to influence us and our families. This filthiness will defile a believer's spirit, soul, and body and destroy our lives.

Believers must not engage in any impure lifestyle or any kind of moral filthiness, including filthy language, obscenity through videos, television, or the internet, which grieves the Holy Spirit and violates God's Holy standards for his people. All Christian believers must take righteousness and holiness of life seriously; the Lord said: "Be Holy for I am Holy." Our houses must be swept clean and filled with the word of God and the holiness of Jesus Christ. The Holy Spirit planted the word of God in our hearts, believing Christians must begin their new life in Jesus Christ - being born again through the word of truth. A new life in Christ demands that we get rid of all moral filthiness that offends and grieve the Holy Spirit; the word of God must be part of our very nature; be the doer of the word of God, not the hearer alone. The implanted word of God in our hearts brings us close to God and helps us through our final salvation and the gift of grace.

Our Lord told apostle Peter: "Put your sword back in its place. Jesus Christ said, on the night of our Lord's arrest to his crucifixion to him, for all who draw the sword will die by the sword" (Matthew 26:52)

The Lord did not want anyone to die because of him. He sacrifices himself in order to pay for our past, present, and future sins. In another scripture, apostle James said:

"What causes fights and quarrels among you? Don't they come from your desires that battle within you? You want something but don't get it. You kill and covet, but you cannot have what you want. You quarrel and fight. You do not have because you do not ask God." (James 4:1-2) What causes fighting and quarreling among people? The primary source of quarrels and conflicts in the church centers on a desire for recognition, honor, power, pleasure, money, and superiority. Selfishness and self-desires become more critical than righteousness and the will of God in the life of human beings. When people engage themselves in this type of life, self-centered conflicts are created in the fellowship. Those who are responsible show themselves to be controlled by their sinful nature rather than by the Spirit of God. Our Lord said: "But I tell you that anyone who is angry with his brother will be subject to judgment. Again, anyone who says to his brother, "Raca," is answerable to the Sanhedrin. But anyone who says, "You Fool" will be in danger of the fire of hell" (Matthew 5:22). Our Lord Jesus is not speaking of righteous anger at injustice or holy indignation for hurtful wicked behavior. Christ condemns the vindictive anger that would unjustly desire the death of another. "Raca" means empty-headed fool, or a godless fool in anger and contempt play, indicating a heat attitude that places one in danger of the fire of hell. Our Lord also condemns lustful behavior, which means Jesus Christ's condemnation is not a sudden thought that Satan may place a person's mind or an improper desire that arises suddenly. Instead, it is a wrong thought or desire that is accompanied by the approval of one's will. It is having an immoral desire that would seek fulfillment if the opportunity arose.

The inner desire for illicit sexual immoralities pleasure, if not resisted, is a sin that will cause earthly difficulties in the life of believing Christians. The Lord God almighty is always with us during earthly difficulties if our hearts are clean and call unto him. The scripture revealed: "When you pass through the waters, I will be with you; and when you pass through the rivers, they will not sweep over you. When you walk through the fire, you will not be burned; the flames will not set you ablaze" (Isaiah 43:2). "So do not fear, for I am with you; do not be dismayed for I am your God. I will strengthen you and help you; I will uphold you with my righteous right hand. "(Isaiah 41:10), "But those who hope in the Lord will renew their strength. They will soar on wings like eagles; they will run and not grow weary, they will walk and not be faith" (Isaiah 40:31) We the word of assurance of our Lord again and again in the book of Prophet Isaiah telling all the believing Christians to hope in the Lord our hope in the Lord will renew our strength to trust in him fully with our lives; it involves looking to him as our source of help and grace in time of need and in times of difficulties of this world. Those who hope in the Lord a promised (1) God's strength to revive them in the middle of exhaustion and weakness, of suffering and trials, (2) they will have the ability to rise above their difficulties like an eagle that soars into the sky and (3) They have the ability to run spiritually without being tired, and they will walk steadily forward without fainting when God delays.

God promises that if his people will patiently trust him, he will provide whatever is needed to sustain them constantly.

In the New Testament, believers have also become God's chosen servants; they can, therefore, claim the promises of these words of God through the prophet Isaiah for themselves. Believing Christians must not fear other humans because God is with them to impart the grace and strength they need to face all the wars as well as all life's circumstances. God almighty, through Jesus Christ, his only begotten son, will help them through times of crises as our source of peace and our sustainer, and he will be our divine advocate. God expresses his love for the children of Israel and to us as well today; the benefits of God's love for his children are unending. All the blessings mentioned in this book of Prophet Isaiah apply even more to those who are God's children through faith and trust in Jesus Christ.

God has created and redeemed us; we belong to him, and he knows every one of us by name. We will not be destroyed when we pass through trouble and affliction, for the Lord is always with us. We are precious and honored in his sight and the object of his great love.

The scripture revealed: "Trust in the Lord withal your heart and lean not on your own understanding in all your ways acknowledge him, and he will make your paths straight" (Proverbs 3:5-6) No matter what we are going through in life; the book of Proverbs in the Holy scripture telling us that we should not lean on our own understanding because our own understanding is limited, fallible and subject to error; we must, therefore, be enlightened by go's word and Holy Spirit. To lean on our own understanding, rather than to trust God according to his Word and Spirit, magnifies the human mind while it diminishes the human spirit.

Dependence on human reason rather than trusting God leads to pride and spiritual leanness. Rather than being wise in our own eyes, we should demonstrate our trust in God by asking him continually for wisdom and knowledge of his will in all spheres of our lives. We must acknowledge him in all our plans, decisions, and activities; we should acknowledge God as Lord and his will as our supreme desire. Every day, we must live in a close, trusting relationship with our Lord and Savior, Jesus Christ, always looking to him for our life's direction by prayer and supplication, with praises and thanksgiving. When we Christian believers do this, God promises to make our path straight, leading us to the goal that he assigned for our lives. He will remove all the obstacles, all the blockage, all the troubles, and difficulties and help us to, as well as enable us to make the right choices in all the areas of our lives. There is no war or any form of earthly difficulties that our Lord and Savior, who is a mighty, all-merciful, all-compassionate, loving Savior, cannot take care of; our God is mighty to save forever. Call unto him and put all your troubles and difficulties in his hands; he is waiting, and he will take care of it for you. In another scripture, we read: "Praise be to the God and Father of our Lord Jesus Christ, the Father of compassion and the God of all comfort, who comforts us in all our troubles, so that we can comfort those in any trouble with the comfort we ourselves have received from God" (2nd Corinthians 1: 3-4) the word comfort means, someone who stands beside a person during the time of trouble, rejection affliction; encouraging and helping them in any areas of earthly troubles. God almighty fulfills this role in our lives by sending his children the Holy Spirit to comfort them. Apostle Paul has learned in his many troubles that no suffering, however severe, no matter how it is, cannot separate believers from the care and compassion of our heavenly Father. God occasionally permits troubles in our lives so that we may experience his love and comfort during times of difficulties and, simultaneously, comfort others in their problems. Apostle Paul stresses that Christian believers' lives involve experiencing hardship and sharing in the sufferings, as well as finding comfort through Jesus Christ. Jesus endured suffering on our behalf, meaning that even now, in this age, He continues to empathize and endure difficulties alongside His people due to the impact of sin. Therefore, we must willingly surrender our lives to Him and commit to living for Him—from our time on earth to our eternal existence in heaven.

Chapter 11: Humanity Rejected God

God Almighty has chosen his people to serve him. The scripture revealed: "The Lord saw how great man's wickedness on the earth had become, and that every inclination of the thoughts of his heart was only evil all the time. The Lord was grieved that he had made man on the earth, and his heart was filled with pain" (Genesis 6:6-7). Humanity's character of sin was blatantly manifested in two primary ways:

God Where Are You?

Sexual lust and violence. Humanity's character has not changed up till today; it is still through lust and violence that evil finds unrestrained expression. Today, sexual sins of all kinds and violence are prevalent in human society everywhere in all the nations of this earth. God deals with people personally and is capable of emotional disappointment and reaction against willful sin and rebellion, as well as their rejection of Him.

Looking at the consistencies of atheism and, more importantly, of atheists. Atheists are inconsistent and, therefore, hypocrites because of their freedom of moral responsibility in their way of the materialism of the Universe. They believe that human life is a product of a ruthless struggle for survival between what they need and what is unneeded, laboring to care for themselves in a powerless, victimized, and gloriously inconsistent. Atheists believe that there is no life after death. There is hope for all the atheists and all those who reject God and are far away from him. God almighty can do what we cannot do; if we come to him in prayer for our loved ones who are far away from God, Jesus Christ's power will wake them up from spiritual death to spiritual life in him. All the believing Christians in this world must study the word of God carefully, daily, systematically, sincerely, and thoroughly. The more we study the word, the more we can feed others who do not know God or rejected God on this earth. Moreover, the more we study the word of God and immerse ourselves in it, the more we will be able to advance in sound evangelization of the people of the world.

The Holy Spirit, our heavenly paraclete comforter, and our teacher, will be able to teach us how to convert the souls of atheists into his holy hands.

Even though the human race rejected God, God's disposition changed towards them; his attitude of mercy and patience turned to judgment. Although God's existence, character, and ultimate purposes remain changeless, he remains open and responsive in his dealings with the human race. God does alter his feelings, attitudes, actions, and mind in accordance with a changing response to his will.

This revelation of God as a God who can feel regret and grief makes clear that God exists in a personal and intimate relationship with his creation. He possesses an intense love for the human race and a divine attentiveness to the problems of humanity. In another scripture, we read: "For you are a people holy to the Lord our God. Out of all the people on the face of the earth, the Lord has chosen you to be his treasured possession" (Deuteronomy 14:2). The Lord God Almighty chose his people and anointed them for the purpose worship, and we may learn how to revere the Lord God always. In order to be able to worship God and learn how to revere him properly, they will need to have sobriety and self-control as well as appropriate celebration. The scripture revealed how people rejected and despised the pleasant land; they did not believe his promise. They grumbled in their tents and did not obey the Lord" (Psalm 106:24-25). Even though we know that the love of God endures forever, we still stay away from him.

God's people should individually and collectively confess their shortcomings before the Lord. But people do not recognize their spiritual failure and repent until God allows them to continue to pursue things contrary to his revealed will, such as an unholy vocational ambition, annual love affairs, worldly pleasures, coveting our desires, or ungodly fellowship with unbelievers, which at the end those things have destructive consequence. Another scripture revealed: "You hate my instruction and cast my words behind you: Consider this, you who forget God, or I will tear you to pieces, with none to rescue" (Psalm 50:17, 22). Lord God almighty says to the wicked that they recite his laws and do not follow his covenant. The Lord then gave them a stern warning to their religious hypocrites among his people, threatening to tear to pieces those who pretend to be devoted to him, those who claim to covenant salvation and the blessings of his word, as well as those who at the same time ignore his righteous commands and conform to the ungodliness of a wicked society. They will find no deliverance in the end; such people receive the greater damnation. People of this earth who rejected God, who stayed away from such as those who call themselves atheists, claiming that there is no God, will face damnation.

The scripture revealed: "Come and listen, all you who fear God; let me tell you what he has done for me. I cried out to him with my mouth; his praises were on my tongue. If I had cherished sin in my heart, the Lord would not have listened, but God has surely listened and heard my voice in prayer. Praise be to God which has not rejected my prayer or withheld his love from me" (Psalm 66:16-20). Those who reject God and take pleasure in unrighteousness have no hope of answering their prayers when they call on God.

God wants us to separate ourselves from sin; only then will He respond to us as a father to a son or daughter. The scripture revealed: "The fool says in his heart, there is no God. They are corrupt, their deeds are vile; there is no one who does good" (psalm 14:1-3). The Lord looks down from heaven on the sons of men to see if there are any who understand, any who seek God.

All have turned aside; they have together become corrupt; there is no one who does good, not even one." The fool is a person who lives as if there is no God, people like Atheists. Fools reveal their rebellion against God almighty in two ways. (1) They reject God's revelation, for they do not believe what the Bible says about God; they scorn the moral principles of God's Word and rely on their own ideas to determine what is right and wrong. They have their own moral relativism. (2) They do not seek God, submit to God's word, pray to God, or trust him concerning their daily lives. (3) This Holy scripture describes the depravity of the wicked and teaches that the human race is by nature separated from God. Apostle Paul quotes those first three verses of this psalm to support the truth in the book of Romans, where he says: "All have sinned and fallen short of the glory of God" (Romans 3:23;

10-12). The people of this earth must know God and put their trust in him. The Lord Jesus Christ cares for all those who put their trust in him. When they are facing trials too great to bear, God invites us to cast all our burdens and cares on him. He then bears the weight of our burdens with us and sustains us in every situation. The Holy Spirit has repeated this invitation throughout redemptive history. Jesus Christ, our Lord and Savior, gave this invitation again and again during his earthly ministry.

Apostle Peter, in his Epistle, stated that believers should humble him selves before God, casting all anxiety on him because Christ cares for us. We must also bring all our anxieties to God in our prayers and supplication, promising that the peace of God will guard our hearts and minds. The scripture revealed: "Therefore, as tongues of fire link up straw and as dry grass sink down in the flames so their roots will decay and their flowers blow away like dust; for they have rejected the law of the Lord Almighty and spurned the word of the Holy One of Israel" (Isaiah 5:24) When God's people rejected the Lord there is always consequences because is a sin in the sight of God. Rejecting God's laws and despising his word will result in people being given over to the consequences of their sins of rejection and to Divine punishment.

The scripture revealed in the book of Genesis: "The Lord was grieved that he had made man on the earth, and his heart was filled with pain. So the Lord said, I will wipe mankind, whom I have created, from the face of the earth – men and animals, and creatures that move along the ground; and birds of the air for I am grieved that I have made them. But Noah found favor in the eyes of the Lord" (Genesis 6:6-8). God the Almighty Father, Son, and Holy Spirit was grieved because the people of this earth rejected the love and mercy of God from the beginning of creation to this present time. God was revealed and made himself known as a God who deals with people personally and as a God who is capable of emotion and disappointment and who can react against the willful sin and rebellion of humankind. Grieved means and indicates that because of the tragic sin of the human race, God's disposition was changed towards them; his attitude of mercy and patience turned to one of judgment.

Although God's existence, character, and ultimate purposes remain open and changeless, God does alter his feelings, attitude, actions, and mind in accordance with a changing response to his will. This revelation of God as a God who can feel rejection and grief makes it clear that God exists in a personal and intimate relationship with his creation. He possesses an intense love for humanity and a divine attentiveness to the plight of the human race. We must thank God for his love for all his creations. Help us to worship God in the Spirit of holiness.

The scripture revealed: "You will keep in perfect peace whose mind is steadfast because he trusts in you. Trust in the Lord forever, for the Lord, the Lord, is the rock eternal" (Isaiah26:3-4). All Christian believers must maintain perfect peace and a steadfast mind in order to get close to the Lord. As the world is going to an end, trying and stressful days towards the end of the history of this age occur, God will keep his own people the remnant who remain steadfast and faithful to the Lord, in all perfect peace, in times of trouble believers must continually strive to keep their minds and hearts turned to the Lord in prayer, trust, and hope>. We must place our faith in the Lord because he is a Rock that endures forever; he is our sure and firm foundation. God almighty never forsakes his children in times of earthly trouble: "But Zion said, the Lord has forsaken me, the Lord has forgotten me. Can a mother forget the baby at her breast and have no compassion for the child she has born? Though she may forget, I will not forget you! See, I have engraved you on the palms of my hands; your walls are ever before me" (Isaiah 49:14-16). Our Lord will never forget us or reject us, no matter what we have done. He is the one who gave the children of Israel his word, and he will never go back on his word.

We people of this earth might experience great adversity, and sometimes we might feel alone, abandoned, and forgotten by God, our Father in heaven. God's response gives divine assurance to any and all the believing Christians going through trying times. God's love for humanity is greater than the natural affection of a loving mother for her children; it is, therefore, unthinkable that he will never forget those who are following him faithfully and sincerely, especially in their times of despair and grief. His compassion for us will never fail, regardless of life's circumstances; he watches over us with great tenderness and love, and we may rest in the conviction that Christ Jesus will never leave us. The evidence of God's great love is that he has engraved us on the palms of his own hands, that he can never forget us; the scars on his hands are always before his eyes as a reminder of the great love that he has showered on us and of his desire to care for us. The scripture revealed: "To whom can I speak and give warning? They find no pleasure in it" (Jeremiah 6:10). Also, in another book of Jeremiah, the prophet we read: "The wise will be put to shame; they will be dismayed and trapped. Since they have rejected the word of the Lord, what kind of wisdom do they have? Therefore, I will give their wives to other men and their fields to new owners. From the least to the greatest, all are greedy for gain; prophet and priests alike, all practice deceit" (Isaiah 8:9-10). The people who are ignorant of the Law of God, who do not believe in God, who do not seek God in their life, whose leaders distorted God's word and falsified its message that the people were assured they could sin without condemnation. Christian believers must be aware of pastors and ministers who teach that those who willfully continue in sin and rebellion against God will still inherit salvation, and God's Kingdom is wrong. People get to the point that they don't want to repent or feel that they can never repent from all shame and remorse for sin gone. Many church members today reach the same stage of apostasy when they reject God's words and commit all sorts of abominable sins.

The scripture continues about how people reject God and his word: "Whenever Jehudi had read three or four columns of the scroll, the King cut them off with a scribe's knife and threw them into the firepot, until the entire scroll was burned in the fire" (Jeremiah 36:23) As the King began destroying the Scroll, he was revealing not only his open hostility to prophet Jeremiah's warnings and plea for repentance but also his contempt for God's written words and for the Lord himself. It is essential for our spiritual vitality that we strive to maintain a love and respect for God's written revelation. Even though we may not attempt to destroy it as King Jehoiakim did, we may still find ourselves throwing the word behind our backs by neglecting to read, study, and meditate on its inspired truth and by failing to live by its precepts. Many people are the same today. As soon as they climb the ladder to a high position, they stay away from this of God and do not want you or anyone to mention the name of God around them. They forget that the Lord is the one who provides the Job for them and moves them to high positions. The New Testament report revealed: "What goes into a man's mouth does not make him unclean, but what comes out of his mouth, that is what makes him unclean" (Matthew 15:11). Our Lord Jesus Christ during his earthly ministry was speaking of foods that enter a person but do not affect their Spirit and conscience before God; our Lord was saying that what comes out of our mouth which comes from the heart, people used their mouth

God Where Are You?

to reject God, to put God aside from their lives and later face the consequences of sin and fall into drugs, abusive and all which and alcohol and all the immoral lives of sin.

Scripture revealed: "They made their hearts as hard as flint and would not listen to the Law or to the words that the Lord Almighty had sent by his Spirit through the earlier prophets. So, the Lord Almighty was very angry. When I called, they did not listen; so when they called, I would not listen, says the Lord almighty. I scattered them with a whirlwind among all the nations, where they were strangers.

The land was left so desolate behind them that no one could come or go. This is how they made the pleasant land desolate" (Zechariah 7:12-14). The children of Israel rejected God, who loved them dearly; their hearts were so hard, like flint, which is one of the most complex substances known in the Old Testament times.

God almighty's call by his Spirit through the earlier prophets was for justice, mercy, and compassion, but the people stubbornly refused to obey God. Then, when the judgment of God came upon them, it was too late for them to repent.

What God expects from his people has not changed from the beginning of creation till now, for he desires that we show love and compassion to those who experience various obstacles and trials and to those who are in need. In the gospel of God, the scripture revealed: "To us the verdict; light has come into the world, but man loved darkness instead of light because their deeds were evil. Everyone who does evil hates the light and will not come into the light for fear that his deeds will be exposed. But whoever lives by the truth comes into the light, so that it may be seen plainly that what he has done has been done through God" (John 3:19-21). Those who do not believe in God are in darkness in this world. A fundamental characteristic of the wicked is that they love darkness, which means that they find their happiness and pleasure in sin and immorality.

On the other hand, genuinely born-again persons love righteousness and hate wickedness, and are grieved when they see the unrighteous deeds of depraved people. They take no pleasure in the sensual entertainment or the expression of sinful conduct shown so openly in contemporary society. People hate to come to the light until something happens to them, such as life adversities, trials, and tribulations, and they will start running to the light. The scripture continues: "The true light that gives light to every man was coming into the world. He was in the world, and though the world was made through him, the world did not recognize him. He came to that which was his own, but his own did not receive him" (John 1:9-11). Jesus Christ is the light of the world; the light of Christ Jesus shines in an evil and sinful world that Satan controls. The majority of the people in the world have not accepted his life or light, but the darkness has not mastered it or overcome it. Jesus Christ illuminates all who hear his gospel by imparting a measure of grace and understanding in order that they may freely choose to accept or reject that message. Apart from this light of Christ, there is no other light by which we may see the truth, know the truth, and be saved. The world did not recognize him, the entire people of unbelievers and those who are operating independently of God, his word, and his rule. The world will never recognize Christ; it will remain different to, or an enemy of, Christ and his gospel until the end of the age. The people in the world are the opponents of the Savior in salvation history. The scripture revealed in the book of Acts when our Lord Jesus Christ was speaking to Apostle Paul from heaven on the road to Damascus: "I will rescue you from your own people and from the Gentiles. I am sending you to them to open their eyes and turn them from darkness to light and from the power of Satan to God so that they may receive forgiveness of sins and a place among those who are sanctified by faith in me.) (Acts 26:17-18) Christ Jesus spoke to Apostle Paul from heaven on the road to Damascus when he was going to persecute all the Jewish people and then turned to the Savior. He gave Paul a divine commission concerning what he desires from the preaching of the gospel to the sinners and to the lost because Satan has blinded the eyes of unsaved people in this world to the reality of their loss, and they are perishing in their condition to the truth of the gospel.

    They can be saved by preaching Jesus Christ in the power of the Holy Spirit, which will open their understanding whereby they will turn from the power of Satan, the ruler of the sinful world, and turn to the power of Christ. The proclamation of the gospel in the power of the Spirit will rescue men and women from the power of Satan and bring them into the Kingdom of Jesus Christ in order that they may receive forgiveness of sins – the forgiveness that comes through faith that is based on Christ sacrificial death on the cross. All the believing Christians have a place for those who are sanctified by faith in Christ Jesus. Those who are forgiven are delivered from the dominion of sin and Satan, and they will be indwelt by and baptized in the Holy Spirit and set apart from the world, and the will from then lives unto God in fellowship with all those saved by faith in Christ. Repentance is essential in order to follow Christ. Jesus is the repentant of heat whereby the new believer will have the Holy Spirit dwell in the heart forever from this earth to heaven. Moreover, the believer will be in the light of the Lord everywhere the believer goes and in everything he is doing. Jesus Christ is the life and the light of the world. Believe in him. You have the light and the lives of this. From this earth to heaven, you will never see darkness or stay in darkness; the light of the Lord God almighty will rest upon you wherever you may go forever. You will be able to live a life of rejoicing and happiness because you are in the light of Christ Jesus.

People should stop rejecting God; the scripture revealed: "Salvation is found in no one else, for there is no other name under heaven given to men by which we must be saved" (Acts 4:12). Jesus Christ is the only way;

the only truth, and the only life.

There is no one else who can receive salvation through Jesus Christ. The greatest need of every individual was salvation from sin and from the wrath of God, and we must preach that this need could be met by no one other than the person of Jesus Christ. This truth reveals the exclusive nature of the gospel and the church's heavy responsibility of preaching and teaching the gospel to everyone on this earth.

The church could be at ease if there were other ways to salvation. But according to Christ Jesus himself, there is no hope for anyone apart from salvation through him. This is the basis for the missionary imperative. In the gospel of Luke: "Blessed are you when men hate you when they exclude you and insult you and reject your name as evil, because of the son of man. Rejoice in that day and leap for joy because great is your reward in heaven. For that is how their fathers treated the prophets" (Luke 6:22-23). During Christ's earthly ministry, he was telling his disciples and us today that we should rejoice and leap for joy because of our faithfulness to Jesus Christ and his godly standards; they are criticized and scorned.

Persecution because of righteousness is evidence that believers are in true fellowship with the Lord since Jesus Christ was also treated and hated by the world. In the Old Testament, the children of Israel rejected the prophets and their messages many times. Today's churches should bear in mind that God almighty sent them prophets to call both leaders and the people to lives of righteousness, faithfulness to the holy scripture, and separation from the world of sin. Many people and some churches are doing the same thing that the Israelites did, rejecting the words of their prophets and breaking the covenant with God along with its blessings of salvation. On the other hand, people today can accept God's message, draw back from sin, deepen their loyalty to God and his word, and continue as God's people. God himself will ultimately reject those churches that reject God's true prophets. Satan can deliberately send false prophets, pastors, and ministers into the churches. The prophets who reject the absolute authority of God's word and claim to have authority equal to God's word and maintain that their revelation is infallible and their words immune from judgment by the church, these false prophets must be firmly rejected. The scripture revealed: "Therefore, he who rejects this instruction does not reject man, but God, who gives you his Holy Spirit" (1st Thessalonian 4:8). Those who reject the instructions of the apostle on sanctification and purity are rejecting God. To disregard Apostle Paul's admonition is to stand squarely against the Holy Spirit and the purity that God desires. God will judge and punish church members who disregard moral purity and instead pursue the satisfaction of their own lust. All those people in the world and within the visible church who reject the truth and instead have delighted in wickedness will be brought to full accountability when Christ Jesus returns for his saints. The disobedient and the ungodly will suffer destruction, wrath, punishment, and condemnation when the Lord Jesus Christ returns from heaven in blazing fire to punish all who do not obey those of God to salvation.

The scripture revealed: "Your word is a lamp to my feet and a light for my path" (psalm 119:105). The word of God is a light for our path on this earth. Wherever we go, we must use the word of God, eat the word of God with the food we eat daily three times a day, drink the word of God with the water that we drink, and breathe the word of God with the air we are breathing in the word of God with the air we are breathing every minute, and every second. God's word contains the spiritual principles that will help us to avoid many adversities, sorrow, pitfalls, and tragedies that might come to us or be brought to us by wrong decisions and choices; consequently, we must treasure its wisdom and steadfastly hold onto its precepts in all life's situations. All Christian believers must hold onto the word of God.

Chapter 12: Humanity Does Not Want To Know God

Many people, millions in the entire world, believe that life ends when they die. They believe that there is no God, and there is no afterlife, and there is no divine heavenly place or eternal life. Atheism is growing more and more every day in the nations of the earth. There are more atheists around the world than ever before, and they continue to grow. Many people become Atheists because of the way they were brought up or because of their education or parental advice; simply get used to what their parents hand over to them. Many people believe that staying away from God and the things of God is the best way to live. At the same time, some people are still searching for God in their own way. Humankind has been unrighteous from birth. The Scripture revealed: "The Lord smelled the pleasing aroma and said in his heart: never again will I curse the ground because of man, even though every inclination of his heart is evil from childhood" (Genesis 8:21a). The Lord God Almighty states the truth about the corruption and depravity of human nature. Humanity is very unrighteous; in other words, sinfulness is considered a property of human nature. After the fall of Adam and Eve, it is clearly concluded that all human beings are born to be sinners since they are all born into adamhood and sin, which is regarded as a property of humanity. The inclination towards malevolence is believed to be inherent in human nature, manifesting itself from an early age, possibly during childhood or youth. The Scripture revealed: "As it is written: There is no one righteous, not even one; there is no one who understands, no one who seeks God.

All have turned away; they have become worthless together; no one does good, not even one. Their throats are open graves; their tongues practice deceit. The poison of vipers is on their lips. Their mouths are full of cursing and bitterness. Their feet are swift to shed blood; ruin and misery mark their ways, and the way of peace they do not know. "Romans

3:10-18 emphasizes the absence of the fear of God in individuals. Those who choose to remain uninformed or distant from the ways of God require a proper understanding of human nature." All people, in their natural state, are sinners. Their entire being is adversely affected by sin and inclined toward conformity to the world and their sinful nature. There is no fear of God in their heart and before their eyes. If they had the fear of God, they would have reached out and sought reconciliation and peace with God. Instead, they continue their life in a deplorable emptiness, full of all manner of immoralities. They all possess a sinful nature that draws them toward sin and evil. The result is that all are guilty and stand under the condemnation of God. God will respond and answer them; if they call unto him in tragic situations, he will offer them forgiveness for their sins and the resurrection of their body.

The Scripture revealed: "The heart is deceitful above all things and beyond cure.

Who can understand it? I the Lord search the heart and examine the mind, to reward a man according to his conduct, according to what his deeds deserve" (Jeremiah 17:9-10). The Lord God, all mighty Father of all mercies, sustainers of all things, stated that the heart is more deceitful than all else desperately sick; without God, the heart is empty and useless; the heart is the inner being of a person and it includes one's desires, feelings and thoughts. Above all, it is desperately evil and corrupt; as a result, humankind turns to selfishness and evil rather than to turn to God's way of righteousness. The corrupt human heart is beyond cure and cannot be changed by itself. The only remedy is to experience the grace of God and be born again through faith in Jesus Christ, whereby receiving a new heart, a new mind, a new spirit – one that hates evil things and delights in following God and delights in doing God's will.

The Scripture revealed: "Worship the Lord your God, and his blessing will take away sickness from among you, and none will miss-carry or be barren in your land, I will give you a full life span" (Exodus 23: 25-26) The Lord God is calling those who reject Him, those who feels there is no God to come to him every day. God almighty connected the removal of sickness, an illness that plagues the people and troubles them with sickness, their wholehearted devotion to him, and their separation from the ungodly influences around them.

People of this earth should not conclude, however, that an individual's sickness necessarily indicates that they have conformed to the wicked ways of society. We people are in the world; worldliness as a whole will cause God to withdraw a portion of his blessing and power from them, affecting even the righteous among the people of God. When people are away from God and don't want anything to do with God, all sorts of earthly problems will start to rule them. They get under Satan's rule, and he can do whatever he wants with them. The Scripture reveals: "No weapon forged against you will prevail, and you will refute every tongue that accuses you.

This is the heritage of the servants of the Lord, and this is their vindication from me, declared the Lord" (Isaiah 54:17). Lord God Father, son, and Holy Spirit comfort Jerusalem, as he would comfort a person, by describing the peace, righteousness, and glory of the restored remnant individual in the future; this is the imagery in describing the conditions of the New Jerusalem. These words bring comfort to believers who are experiencing great afflictions or adversity. When they are weighed down by trials and shaken by the storms of life's circumstances, they must remember that these conditions cause our Lord to have compassion on us and draw near to us so that we may be spiritually strengthened. God invited all who forsake him to return to him and be restored to fellowship and blessing

g. Jesus Christ is calling from the Old Testament to the New Testament. He said: "Come, all you who are thirsty, come to the waters; and you who have no money, come, buy and eat! Come; buy wine and milk without money and without cost. Why spend money on what is not bread and your labor on what does not satisfy? Listen, listen to me, and eat what is good; your soul will delight in the richest fare. Give ear and come to me; hear me that your soul may live. I will make an everlasting covenant with you, my faithful love promised to David" (Isaiah 55:1-3). The Lord God Almighty Father continues to call the sinners and the lost, people of all other religious, pagan, and idol worshipers, to himself in order that their souls may live. This is an essential prerequisite for salvation. It is a genuine spiritual hunger and thirst for forgiveness and for a right relationship with God, the Father, based on the sacrificial death of the servant, the Messiah. People must repent from their sins and draw near to God in faith; hunger and thirst for God's righteousness and the power of his kingdom are vital conditions for receiving the fullness of his Holy Spirit. In another Scripture, read about the word of assurance of God that says: "The Lord is my Rock, my fortress, and my deliverer; my God is my Rock, in whom I take refuge. He is my shield and the horn of my salvation, my stronghold. I call to the Lord, who is worthy of praise, and I am saved from my enemies" (Psalm 18:2-3). Our Lord is our stronghold and shield in all the storms of life.

Jesus Christ is the Rock that never

moves and never changes. All Christian believers struggling against this world's physical and spiritual forces must know that God is their Rock, their fortress, and their only deliverer. God Almighty cares for us; He created us in His own image; He came down from heaven to buy us with His own precious blood and deliver us from sin so that we may live and have life in Him, a new life, life in the spirit of the Trinitarian God. Christ Jesus is our Rock – he provided safety and security with his immovable strength.

Christ is our stronghold and our fortress; Jesus is our place of refuge and safety where the enemy cannot penetrate or conquer. Jesus Christ is our only deliverer - he is a living protector, forever living the everlasting Lord. Jesus Christ is our shield – He is God the Son who stepped between us, made us children of God, and blessed us with the gift of salvation, strength, and victories, power to deliver and save us; our high tower among the rocks He is the one who saves us from plunder and all the earthly destruction. The Lord Jesus Christ gives us strength to his people that call unto him every minute and every time our Lord and Savior blesses his people with joy unspeakable and peace. The Scripture revealed: "The Lord your God is with you, he is mighty to save. He will take great delight in you, he will quiet you with his love, he will rejoice over you with singing" (Zechariah 3:17). Our Lord God Almighty Father in whom all life dwell is a singing God who delights to lavish love upon all the redeemed. He is a loving, compassionate God full of truth and righteousness. The Scripture says: "Finally, be strong in the Lord and in his mighty power. Put on the full armor of God so that you can take your stand against the Devil's schemes.

For our struggle is not against flesh and blood but against the rulers, against the authorities, against the powers of this dark world, and against the spiritual forces of evil in the heavenly realms. Therefore, put on the full armor of God so that when the day of evil comes, you may be able to stand your ground, and after you have done everything, to stand"(Ephesians 6:11-13). All the believing Christians are engaged in a spiritual conflict with evil. This spiritual conflict is described as warfare of faith that continues until we enter the life to come. Satan is a master minder and masterful strategist who seeks believers' downfall through his schemes. Some of the Devil's schemes are to perpetrate division in the family, with husband and wife, and especially in the church. He will cause and form any causes that bring unbelief in the promises of God, discouragement, temptation to sin, compromise of conscience, unforgiveness, making people get their eyes and focus out of Jesus Christ, creating fear, accusation, indulging our sinful nature, spiritual apathy and so forth. Apostle Paul instructs believers to take their stand against the Devil's schemes.

Believing Christians must take confidence in the fact that Christ Himself has secured our victory through his death on the cross. Christ Jesus waged a triumphant battle against Satan, disarmed the evil powers and authorities, led captive in his train, and redeemed the believer from Satan's power.

At this present time, we are involved in a spiritual warfare that we fight by the power of the Holy Spirit against the sinful desires within ourselves as well as against the ungodly pleasures of the world and against the temptations of every pleasure of Satan and his evil forces. All the believing Christians are called to be separate from the present world system and to hate its evil, resisting and overcoming its temptations and sin. As Christian soldiers, we must wage war against all the evil forces in the world, not in our own power but with the spiritual weapons of the Holy Spirit. In our warfare of faith, we are called to endure hardships like good soldiers of Jesus Christ, ready to suffer for the gospel;

fight the good fight of the faith, wage war and persevere, conquer, and be victorious, triumph, defend the gospel, contend for the faith, not to fear or be frightened by the threat of the opponents, most important put on the full armor of God; stand strong and firm in the Lord; destroy all Satan's strongholds take captive of every negative thought and become mighty in battle. All the believing Christians are faced with a spiritual conflict with Satan and a host of evil spirits called the power of darkness, which are the spiritual forces of evil that energize the ungodly, who also oppose the will of God in the life of people and frequently attack the believing Christians of this world. This constitutes a great multitude and is organized into an empire of evil with rank and order.

God Where Are You?

The Scripture continues: "Take the helmet of salvation and the sword of the Spirit, which is the word of God. And pray in the spirit on all occasions with all kinds of prayers and requests. With this in mind, be alert and always pray for all the saints" (Ephesians 6:17-18). The sword of the spirit is the word of God, which is our offensive weapon in spiritual warfare. Satan will make every effort to undermine or destroy a believer's confidence in that sword, if possible, which is the word of God, which is alive forever because the word of God is God. The church must defend the inspiring scriptures against allegations that scripture is not God's sword in everything it teaches. To abandon the attitude of Jesus and the apostles toward God's inspired word is to destroy its power to rebuke or correct, to redeem, to heal, to drive out demons, and to overcome all evil. To deny the Scripture's absolute trustworthiness in all it teaches is to deliver ourselves into Satan's hand. All Christian believers must pray in the spirit; our warfare against Satan's spiritual forces calls for an intensity in prayer, praying fervently, praying in the spirit on all and every occasion with all kinds of prayers, for all the saints of God on earth and for all the government and people in all the nations and for individuals. Believers must keep on praying. Prayer is not to be seen just as another weapon but as part of the actual strong weapon and most important weapon in conflict; it is where the victory is won for us and others by working together with God almighty himself. To hail to pray or stop praying diligently, with all kinds of prayers in all situations and in all circumstances, is to surrender to the power of the enemy. We must know that there is God in heaven. Nothing happens without his order. He is the creator, no one else; no other God is beside him. The scripture said: "Finally brothers, whatever is true, whatever is noble, whatever is right, whatever is pure, whatever is lovely, whatever is admirable – if anything is excellent or praiseworthy, think about such things. And the peace of God, which transcends all understanding, will guard your hearts and your minds in Christ Jesus. Whatever you have learned or received or heard from me or seen in me, put it into practice. And the God of peace will be with you" (Philippians 4:7-9). In all the areas of the believing Christians, the peace of God will guard our hearts and minds when we call on God the Father, God the Son, and God the Holy Spirit from hearts that remain in Christ Jesus and in his word; then the God of peace which surpasses, that transcends all understanding will flood our trouble souls. This peace is an inner tranquility mediated by the Holy Spirit; it involves a firm conviction that Jesus Christ is near and that God's love will be active in our lives for good. When we lay our troubles before God in prayer, this peace will stand guard at the door of our hearts and minds, preventing the cares and heartaches of life from upsetting our lives and determining our hope in Jesus Christ. If fear and anxiety return, prayer, petition, and thanksgiving will once again place us under the peace of God that guards our hearts and minds. There, we are safe and rejoice in the Lord. Whatever is pure and admirable comes from God to experience peace in Jesus Christ that transcends all understanding and freedom from anxiety; believers must fix their minds on those things that are true, noble, right, holy, and pure; if believers do these things, the peace of God will be with them forever according to the teaching and preaching of apostle Paul to the Philippians. The consequence of fixing our minds on the unholy and impure things of the world is that the joy of God's nearness and peace is lost, and our hearts and minds are no longer guarded with the peace of God.

The Scripture clearly revealed the sword of God on unbelievers: "The wrath of God is being revealed from heaven against all the godlessness and wickedness of men who suppress the truth by their wickedness. Sin, what may be known about God, is plain to them because God has made it plain to them.

For since the creation of the world, God's invisible qualities, His eternal power, and divine nature have been clearly seen, being understood from what has been made, so that men are without excuse. For although they know God, they neither glorified him as God nor gave thanks to him, but their thinking became futile, and their foolish hearts were darkened.

Although they claimed to be wise, they became fools and exchanged the glory of the immortal God for images made to look like mortal man and birds and animals and reptiles. Therefore, God gave them over in the sinful desires of their hearts to sexual impurity for the degrading of their bodies with one another.

They exchanged the truth of God for a lie and worshiped and served created things rather than the creator who is forever praised. Amen, because of this, God gave them over to shameful lust. Even their women exchanged natural relations for unnatural ones.

In the same way, the men also abandoned natural relations with women and were inflamed with lust for one another.

Men committed indecent acts with other men and received in themselves the due penalty for their perversion.

Furthermore, since they did not think it worthwhile to retain the knowledge of God, he gave them over to a depraved mind to do what ought not to be done. They have become filled with every kind of wickedness, evil, greed, and depravity. They are full of envy, murder, strife, deceit and malice. Slanderers, God-hates, insolent, arrogant, and boastful; they invent ways of doing evil; they disobey their parents; they are senseless, faithless, heartless, and ruthless. Although they know God's righteous decree that those who do such things deserve death, they not only continue to do these very things but also approve of those who practice them" (Romans 1:28-32). People of this world who do not want to know God, those who reject God, such as Atheists, pagans, and idol worshipers, fall under Satan's rules.

Summary

The unregenerate people who rejected God in their life, the Idol worshipers, Pagans, Atheists, and all the false prophets in this world, are living under the rules of Satan and his Devil's angels; some of them are even under the demonic bondages in so many ways on this earth. They are proud and always seek honor and exalt themselves rather than give glory to God. They are full of all forms of immoral, Impurity, and shameful lusts. If they do not turn around and repent, they will ultimately be given over to a depraved mind. People who reject God continue in their shameful lust and sin. They also justify their actions as a common human weakness, persuading themselves that they are still in fellowship with the Holy Spirit, possess salvation, and still go to heaven. They blindfolded themselves with the word of God in the Holy Scripture, where the scripture made it clear that no immoral, impure, greedy, or wicked person can inherit the kingdom of God. God almighty Father gave them over to all their evil ways of life. God's abandonment of any society or individual people is that they become obsessed with sexual immorality and perversion. God gave them over, which means that God abandoned these persons to intensified lusts – sinful desires, a lust for sexual immorality pleasure.

God's abandonment means that God

gives them over to sinful sexual pleasure that degrades and destroys the body with one another. God gave them over to sinful sexual pleasure that degrades and destroys the body with one another. God gives them over to a depraved mind; their minds justify their unrighteous actions, and they become continually preoccupied with evil and the pleasure of sinful desires. God gives them over because they all reject the truth of God's revelation and seek pleasure in ungodliness. God almighty Rather has two purposes in abandoning the unrighteous to sin: to allow sin and its consequences of sin to accelerate as part of his judgment on them and to make them realize their need for salvation. God gave them up because they believed the lie of Satan, the father of lies, who told them, "They will be like

God" (Genesis 3:5). Humanity's propensity to believe the lie and seek to determine its destiny apart from God a always leads to some form of idolatry for instance, greed, and materialism, whereby, the scripture incessantly warns against pride. "In the pride of your heart you say I am god" (Ezekiel 28:2). They do not seek God or want to know God; God gave them up; men with other men, women with other women, homosexual abomination is key evidence of human degeneracy resulting from believing Satan's lie. God gave society over to the consequences of deception. Any nation that justifies homosexuality or lesbianism as an acceptable lifestyle is at an advanced stage of moral corruption because the Holy Scripture warned about this horrible activity. God almighty will never approve those who practice them. One of human sinfulness is God's condemnation of a condition equally as severe as the practice itself, approving the immoral and perverted practice of others. Sin is in the sense of taking pleasure in the immoral actions of others as dramatized in books, cinema, videos, pornography, and Television entertainment. The vicarious enjoyment of lust and evil in entertainment is therefore condemned. We know what harm is produced by the portrayal of immorality that dominates the entertainment media because many people derive pleasure in watching other people committing sin and engage in ungodly actions, even while abstaining brings you under the same judgment as those engaging in such evil practices.

Sin is intensified in any society wherever

it meets with no inhibition from the disapproval of others. Those who profess faith in Jesus Christ and who use the immoral actions of others for entertainment and enjoyment are directly contributing to public opinion favorable to immortality. Therefore, the corruption and eternal damnation of an indefinite number of other people. Sin must be exposed and judged on the day of final judgment; all who have not believed the truth but have delighted in wickedness will be condemned, according to Apostle Paul to the Thessalonian church. Delighting in wickedness while refusing the word and the love, as well as the truth of God, will be the deciding factor in the judgment of God on the last day.

Those who are destined to experience

God's wrath will be those who did not love the truth and, therefore, participated in and entertained themselves with evil and immorality. They will be given over by God to judgment, which includes demonic deception and the power of darkness. Those who are experiencing condemnation during the "day of the Lord" will include not only the world of unbelievers but also those guilty of turning away from the true faith. They choose the pleasure of sin instead of enjoying God, and they are swept along with the tide of the world on the last day. Many people reject God during times of illness, disease, trials, troubles, problems, and all life difficulties; the word of God must be the source of supernatural help. They must not give up to any earthly challenges no matter what the physician's diagnosis or what type of financial problem it is; God the almighty Father Jesus Christ, his only begotten Son, Holy Spirit the giver of life who proceeds from the Father and the Son, glorified and worship; promises us greater things in store, he filled our future with promises and hope. The word of God healing with his strength in us encourages us and comforts us as we focus on our Lord's healing power. He will heal our illnesses and diseases, solve all our earthly problems, and make us one in him. Jesus Christ is knocking. Let us open the door of our hearts and let him in so that he, the Father, and the Holy Spirit will abode in us. Therefore, why do we always ask, where is God? If we believe in him, he is always here, and He always will be. The scripture revealed: "Then you will call upon me and come and pray to me, and I will listen to you. You will seek me and find me when you seek me with all your heat. I will be found by you, declares the Lord, and will bring you back from captivity. I will gather you from all the nations and places where I have banished you, declares the Lord, and will bring you back to the place from which I carried you into exile" (Jeremiah 29:12-14). This scripture not only applied to the Israelites alone, but it applied to all the people on this earth who rejected, put God aside, and made themselves god. There is always a strategic timing that is often involved in the fulfillment of God's promises. God will fulfill his word and promises both in relation to the fullness of his redemptive purpose and in response to his faithful people's earnest prayers. God almighty wants his children to seek him in prayer with all their hearts, spirits, souls, and bodies. God promised that if they sought him, they would find him. God will listen, answer from heaven, and fulfill his promises of restoration. God always desires to do great things for his people. He moves his people to great praying, and the timing of God's answers to their prayers is often linked to God's purposes for his people as a whole in the world. In the Book of Deuteronomy, the Lord God said: "There you will worship man-made gods of wood and stone, which cannot see or hear or eat or smell.

But if from there you seek the Lord your God, you will find him if you look for him with all your heart" (Deuteronomy 4:28-29). Awareness of who God is in this universe is fundamental to every human being. To find

God and to know him in his fullness, a person must be able to seek him with passion and with wholehearted devotion. Knowing God and experiencing the power of God, his blessings, and the righteousness of his kingdom does not come easily; it will happen only to those who diligently and earnestly seek God and desire his nearness, the fullness of his spirit, and his gift of eternal life. In another Scripture, God said: "And you, my son Solomon, acknowledge the God of your father, and serve him with wholehearted devotion and with a willing mind, for the Lord searches every heart and understands every motive behind the thoughts. If you seek him, he will be found by you, but if you forsake him, He will reject you forever." (1st Chronicles 28:9) This was King David's charge of instruction to his son

Solomon in the Old Testament. David instructed that if his son Solomon acknowledged God the Father, served him, and sought him with wholehearted devotion and a faithful, willing mind, he would find him. Acknowledgment of God means to have practical knowledge of his person and ways and to live in a close relationship or fellowship with him and with his word.

We must desire to serve God, which means to desire the grace of God, which is in Christ Jesus our Lord and Savior, his Kingdom power, and his righteousness to such an extent that we continually pray for his active presence in our lives and earnestly seek to obey his will for our live, we must be feeling hungering and thirsting for his righteousness. Giving thanks for everything that is happening in our lives, either good or bad, because it would have been worse if we did not have him.

Get close to the Lord in the time of earthly difficulties instead of continue asking questions: "Where is God in the adversities of life?" Call unto him; he will answer your call at any time!!!

Prayer For Unbelievers And Believers

In this Holy Scripture, we have the word of God revealed to all the people of this earth; God almighty called all the people and said: "Seek the Lord while he may be found; call on him while he is near. Let the wicked forsake his way and the evil man his thoughts. Let him turn to the Lord, and he will have mercy on him, and to our God, for he will freely pardon" (Isaiah 55: 6-7). People of this Universe must seek God while he may be found; they must still keep the promise of his response. God's time of salvation is limited; a day is coming when he will refuse to be found. Lord God, almighty compassionate, gracious father full of truth and righteousness abounding in love and forgiveness. Jesus Christ, his only begotten Son, full of grace and truth, the Holy Spirit, forever one God. Let those who do not know you seek you and find you; let them give their life to you in spirit and truth worship you; give their life to you faithfully and truthfully. Let those who seek you find you when people call unto you sincerely, look down from heaven, and answer their prayers. Touch the hearts of unrepentant souls and turn them around on to you. Let them leave their lives of abomination, wickedness, impurity, and immoral life and put on Christ, who can wash them clean from any unrighteousness and bless them with a new life in him. When the sinners pray to you, answer their prayers, our Lord.

Those who say there is no God, reveal yourself to them in the simplest way, in a miraculous way. Let them know there is God; you're the only creator of heaven and earth, sea, and everything that dwells in it. Let the gospel reach the unreachable in their language and be converted unto you, our Lord. Let the Atheists, Idol worshipers, and Pagans know there is God; let them seek you, find you, and stop worshiping the creation, but worship the creator who lives forever more.

In the mighty Holy name of Jesus Christ, I pray, amen. Let the sacrifices of prayer, praises, and thankfulness continually flow from our hearts, minds, spirits, souls, and bodies to your throne every minute and every second for what you have done for us on this earth, what you are doing for us past, present time and what you are still going do for us in future, until you come again to set up your Kingdom of peace righteousness and love. I pray this in the mighty holy name of our Savior Jesus Christ, who is at the right hand of God, who reigns in the unity of the Holy Spirit, one God, forever and ever. Amen. Our Lord and Savior help us to open the door of evangelization of the gospel of Godin all the nations of the earth and under the earth so that those who sit in the shadow of darkness will see the light and follow the light and forever stay in the light. Make those who are spiritually dead and do not know the things of God alive in you, my Lord; touch their hearts, spirits, souls, body and make them alive in you. In the mighty Holy Name of Jesus Christ, I pray Amen. God put pride down on all Atheists, touch their stubborn heat, convict them of the sin of unbelief and pride, and show yourself to them by revealing to them the Holy Scriptures because if they do not know that God exists, they also do not know that there is life after death. Pray for all atheists, our Lord, the prayer that cannot be uttered.

Send your word from heaven and convert their souls into your holy hands. We pray that You have mercy on all the Atheists' souls, spirits, and bodies and grant them everlasting life and peace through Jesus Christ, our Lord. Amen.

God Where Are You?

Song Of God of Creation

—Margaret Clarkson, 1987

God of creation, all-powerful, all-wise,
Lord of the universe, rich with surprise,
Maker, Sustainer, and Ruler of all,
We are your children—you hear when we call.

God of the ages, through time's troubled years,
You are the one in whom hist'ry coheres;
Nations and empires your purpose ful-fill,
Moving in freedom, yet working your will.

God of redemption, who wrought our rebirth,
Called out your church from the ends of the earth,
Still, you are Savior, put darkness to flight;

Grace Dala Bolagun

Overcome sin by salvation's pure light.

God of your people, your Word still stands fast;
Do for us now as you've done in the past!
Yours is the kingdom, your triumph we claim,
Challenging evil in Jesus' strong name.

God of our now, all our trust is in you,
Covenant God, ever faith-ful and true;
Sov'reign Creator, Redeemer, and Lord,
Now and forever your name be adored!

Revelation Of Lord

"The revelation of Jesus Christ, which God gave him to showed his servants what must soon take pace. He made it known by sending his angel to his servant John, who testifies to everything he saw that is, the word of God and the testimony of Jesus Christ. Blessed is the one who reads the words of this prophecy, and blessed are those who hear it and take to heart what is written in it, because the time is near."

Revelation 1:1-3

Grace Dala Bolagun

ORDER FORM

To order your copy of any book:

Name: _____

Address: _____

_____

Telephone: _____

Fax#: _____

Mail: _____

Quantity: _____

Mail To: Grace Religious Books Publishing & Distributors, Inc. New York
248 Lombard Street 2nd Fl.
New Haven, CT 06513.

About the Author

Grace Dola Balogun graduated from Fordham University Graduate School of Religion and Religious Education in the year 2010 with an M.A. in Religion and Religious Education. She has been a prayer mentor and advisor for many Christians of all denominations for many years.

Visit her online at:
http://www.Gracereligiousbookspublishers.com
Facebook:
https://www.facebook.com/grace.d.balogun
Twitter: https://twitter.com/prayersource

To order additional copies of this book, please E-mail:

Grace Dala Bolagun

info@gracereligiousbookspublishers.com.

This book is available for purchase through 30,000 wholesalers, retailers, and bookstores across the United States, Canada, and more than 100 countries worldwide. To arrange an interview or inquire about speaking engagements with Grace Dola Balogun, please reach out via email at info@gracereligiousbookspublishers.com

Other Books by the Same Author

Prayer: The Source of Strength for Life Published August 2nd, 2011.

The Cross and the Crucifixion Published December 13th, 2011.

Spirit Power, Volume I Published December 6th, 2011.

Spirit Power, Volume II Published December 6th, 2011.

La Oracion Fuente de Fortaleza Para la Vida Published September 9th, 2011.

Three Simple Solutions for World Peace Published August 31st, 2012.

Justification by Faith Alone in Christ Alone Published November 27th, 2012.

Prayer for the Bully Victims and the Bully too published December 24th, 2012.

"She must be Silent" Published June 13th, 2013.

God's Predestination Published August 20th, 2014.

Christ The Consummation of Peace Forever Published December 2014.

Jesus Christ The Only Way to Heaven, The Only Truth, The Only Life 2022.

Light From Heaven Daily Devotional Prayer Study Guide August 2020.

The Trinitarian Activity of Love from Beginning of Creation 2022.

The Unchangeable God Volume I & II Published Feb. 2023 etc.

On sale at Amazon .com, Barns & Noble and all other Book Stores in the United Kingdom and around the world.

www.ingramcontent.com/pod-product-compliance
Lightning Source LLC
Chambersburg PA
CBHW061757070526
44586CB00023B/2611